# SECURE

## 90 DAYS TO A MORE CONNECTED RELATIONSHIP

MATT WADE

For permission requests, please contact:
Matt Wade
c/o Unstuck
204 N. Main Street, Suite 6
Dickson, TN 37055
www.unstucktherapy.org

ISBN: 9798218584238
First Edition
Printed in the United States of America
Publication Date: February 2026

Cover design by @benayoubdz
Interior design by HMD Publishing

Published by Unstuck
Distributed via IngramSpark

# DISCLAIMERS

The information presented in *Secure* by Matt Wade is for general informational purposes only. While every effort is made to provide up-to-date and accurate content, no representations or warranties of any kind, express or implied, are made about the completeness, accuracy, reliability, or suitability of the information provided. Any reliance you place on this material is strictly at your own risk.

In no event will Matt Wade be liable for any loss or damage, including but not limited to indirect or consequential loss, or any loss arising from the use of this information, including data loss or financial loss.

Throughout *Secure*, you may find links to other websites that are not under our control. We have no influence over the nature, content, or availability of those sites. The inclusion of any links does not imply a recommendation or an endorsement of the views expressed within them.

Every effort is made to keep content referenced in *Secure* available and accessible. However, we take no responsibility for, and will not be liable for, any temporary unavailability due to technical issues beyond our control.

Every effort has been made to accurately represent the products and services in this workbook. There is no guarantee that you will achieve specific results by following the ideas in these materials. Examples provided are not to be interpreted as promises or guarantees.

Your level of success in attaining results depends on several factors, including your background, motivation, commitment, and actions. Since these factors vary from person to person, we cannot guarantee success, nor are we responsible for any individual outcomes. Results may vary.

## DISCLOSURE OF RESOURCES

Some of the links in this workbook may be affiliate links. This means that if you click on a link and make a purchase, you are responsible for that purchase, and no refunds can be provided. Regardless, we only recommend products or services we personally use and believe will add value to our readers. This disclosure is made in accordance with the Federal Trade Commission's 16 CFR, Part 255: *Guides Concerning the Use of Endorsements and Testimonials in Advertising*.

## MEDICAL DISCLAIMER

The content of this workbook is provided for general informational purposes only and is not intended as, nor should it be considered, a substitute for professional medical advice. Do not use this material to diagnose or treat any medical condition. If you have or suspect a medical issue, please contact a qualified healthcare provider promptly.

## MENTAL HEALTH DISCLAIMER

This workbook is not intended to replace professional mental health care. Do not use this content to diagnose or treat any mental health condition. If you are experiencing emotional or psychological distress, please contact a licensed mental health professional.

While Matt Wade is the creator of this workbook, *Secure* is designed for educational and experiential purposes only. It does not establish or imply a therapeutic relationship or provide clinical advice, nor does it replace couples' or individual therapy.

# SAFETY

Safety is everything in a coupleship – whether this be emotionally, physically, financially, mentally, spiritually, or socially. While this workbook is designed to help couples strengthen their relationships, it is important to acknowledge that no relationship should involve or endure any form of abuse, harm or manipulation. If you or your partner is experiencing any type of abuse, it is essential to prioritize safety and seek professional help before engaging in this workbook.

**If you are unsure about abuse or harm, here are the types to consider**

- Physical Abuse: Any intentional use of physical force that causes injury or harm.

- Emotional Abuse: Manipulation, intimidation, constant criticism, humiliation, or any behavior that erodes your sense of self-worth.

- Verbal Abuse: Name-calling, yelling, belittling, or any kind of hurtful language directed at you.

- Sexual Abuse: Any form of unwanted sexual activity, coercion, or manipulation into sexual acts.

- Financial Abuse: Controlling your access to financial resources or limiting your ability to work or make financial decisions.

- Digital Abuse: Using technology to harass, stalk, or control your online activities, such as through monitoring or threatening messages.

- Spiritual Abuse: Using religious beliefs or spiritual practices to control or manipulate your actions or feelings.

If you find yourself in a relationship where any of these forms of abuse are present, please know that it is not your responsibility to "fix" the relationship alone. Your safety is the most important thing, and help is available.

**Get Help:**

If you or someone you know is in an abusive relationship, please contact the **National Domestic Violence Hotline** at **1-800-799-7233** or visit **www.thehotline.org** for support.

You deserve to feel safe, valued, and respected. If you are unsure or confused about what constitutes abuse, reaching out to a trusted professional or calling a hotline can provide clarity and support.

# CONTENTS

# DEDICATION

To the select couples who walked this 90-day journey with me:
Your honesty, courage, and willingness to do the work made this
project come alive. Your insights and vulnerability didn't just
refine this workbook — they made it more human, more hopeful,
and far more *secure*.

*"In your arms, I find my peace,*
*where heart & soul release;*
*together we heal, together we grow,*
*a love that roots us deep below."*

While *Secure* is designed to help couples grow stronger together, it's important to acknowledge that not every relationship is in a place where this type of work is helpful — or even safe.

This workbook is **not** intended for relationships where there is:

- **Ongoing abuse (emotional, physical, sexual, or financial)**
  If either partner feels unsafe, fearful, or controlled, this workbook is not the appropriate tool. Please seek help from a licensed professional, crisis center, or domestic violence organization.

- **Untreated mental illness that disrupts daily functioning**
  Conditions like severe depression, active suicidality, untreated bipolar disorder, or psychosis can significantly affect the ability to engage in this kind of relational work. Individual therapy and stabilization should be prioritized first.

- **Active addiction**
  If one or both partners are struggling with substance abuse or compulsive behaviors, it's essential to seek specialized addiction treatment before engaging in couples work.

- **Unwillingness to participate**
  This workbook only works when both partners are willing. If one person is doing the work while the other is checked out, defensive, or uninterested, it may create more hurt than healing.

- **A current affair or ongoing betrayal**
  If trust has been recently broken through infidelity or deceit, couples therapy may be needed first to establish safety and containment before moving into a workbook like this.

We want you to get the most out of *Secure*, but more importantly, we want you to be safe, supported, and set up for success. If you're unsure whether this workbook is right for your relationship at this time, consider speaking with a trusted therapist, coach, or clinician who can help you assess your next steps.

There's no shame in needing more support — in fact, that's a powerful sign of care for yourself and your relationship. When the time is right, this book will be here waiting for you.

# INTRODUCTION

Over a decade ago, our marriage hit a breaking point. It got ugly—fast. Amber and I found ourselves sitting on the edge of our bed, both in tears, quietly imagining what life would look like if we went our separate ways. The image of our kids splitting holidays between two homes was nauseating. We weren't screaming or blaming each other. We were just… silent. Heartbroken. Empty.

The truth is, we still loved each other. We just didn't know how to live together anymore—at least, I didn't. At the time, I was a campus pastor at one of the fastest-growing churches in America. From the outside, I was thriving. But inside, I was falling apart—depressed, numbing with food and bourbon, forty pounds overweight, my blood pressure rising, and Type II diabetes closing in. My world was collapsing, and I couldn't find a way out.

What we didn't realize then was that we had been drifting for years. Like many couples, we had slipped into what I call *relational drift*—the slow, subtle kind that sneaks up on you. It's like floating in the ocean on a calm day. You feel the sun, the breeze, the gentle waves. Everything seems fine—until you look up and realize you've drifted so far from shore you can't see the land anymore. That's what happened to us.

When our son, Carson, was born, life seemed perfect. I was self-employed, running a growing web and design company, and spent my days surrounded by creativity and fatherhood. I adored those early years with Carson—his giggles, his tiny hands gripping my finger, his visits to my office. We built a bond that felt sacred. But while I was connecting deeply with my son, I was disconnecting at home.

We didn't know what was happening, so we kept going through the motions. Like many of you reading this, we were *pros at pretending*. On the outside, everything looked fine. But something inside me had shifted. I thought it had shifted in Amber too, but I was wrong. She was shocked by how far I had drifted, and I was shocked that she was shocked. It was confusing and painful.

I remember one day in particular—Amber and I were jogging through our neighborhood in Sylvan Park. She asked me something simple, something like, "Why don't you just..." I never heard the rest. My response was sharp, cold, and cruel. I snapped, yelling, "I just wish you would leave me the hell alone!" I can still see the look on her face—the moment I broke her heart for the first time. I could take you to the stop sign where it happened. I drive by it often, and I still feel that sting.

Unfortunately, it wouldn't be the last time I broke her heart.

As the years passed, the distance grew. About ten years into our marriage—around the time our daughter, Nellie, was born—we hit another wall. Looking back, it was probably the same wall I had been building since that jog. But this time, it felt unmovable. We were both exhausted, angry, and lost. The wall between us felt impossible to climb.

How did it get so big? Avoidance. Fear. Unhealed childhood wounds. Lies to myself. Shame. A wrecked nervous system. And a lack of the skills to truly communicate.

It took everything in me to face what I had done—to look my wife in the eyes and tell the truth, and lay it all out. The alternative was pretending, hiding, and slowly destroying everything we had left. *But there is no intimacy where there is secrecy.* Healing doesn't happen in hiding. I knew if I didn't come clean, we'd end up disconnected, divorced, and raising kids who never really understood why their home fell apart. Once the truth was out—messy and painful as it was—we could finally start to heal for real.

*There is no intimacy where there is secrecy.*

I remember the first day I walked into our therapist office. Instantly, I made a snap judgment about Kenny. He was an older white

13

guy—white hair, pearl-snap cowboy shirt, and worn-out boots that had seen some years. My first thought? *This is who they sent us? Some church-budget therapist?* But I couldn't have been more wrong.

Kenny was sharp, compassionate, and funny. Therapy with him was tender, but real. He had this rare ability to be kind without coddling, firm without shaming. He could see right through our defenses and still hold space for us to grow. Healing with him wasn't easy—it was slow, messy, and gut-wrenching. But through that painful, sacred process, we somehow found our way back to each other.

We had to face everything: our childhood wounds, our unhealthy patterns, the walls we built, the stories we told ourselves, and all the ways we stopped being curious about each other. But over time, something miraculous happened. We started to feel safe again. Seen again. Connected again.

More than a decade later—over twenty years into our marriage—Amber and I are stronger than we've ever been. We've become best friends again. Healing wasn't just hard—it was brutal. But it was also holy. Awful and sacred, all at once.

I share a part of our story because I know many of you may be standing in a similar place—confused, disconnected, or scared that it might be too late. Maybe you've tried counseling before and it didn't stick. Maybe you're just now realizing how far the drift has taken you.

Wherever you are, I want you to know:

You're not broken.

You're human.

And with the right tools, you can rebuild.

That's why I created the *Secure* workbook. As both a husband and a therapist, I noticed a gap between the resources available to couples. Some books focused solely on emotion—how we feel, attach, and respond to one another—but offered little direction on what to *do* next. Others were full of practical tools and communication strategies, but they didn't address the deeper emotional needs that keep love from feeling safe.

I wanted to bridge that gap—to create something that spoke to both the heart and the head – in a workbook format. *Secure* was born out of that desire: a 90-day journey designed to help couples connect, understand, and rebuild trust through both emotional depth and practical application.

This workbook draws from the foremost research in relationship science—Sue Johnson's Emotionally Focused Therapy and John and Julie Gottman's work on relational health—along with other evidence-based approaches that honor the complexity of human connection. My hope is that as you move through these pages, you'll not only understand each other more clearly but begin to experience what real safety feels like.

It's not a quick fix—it's a slow return. A return to safety. To honesty. To curiosity. To the love you thought might be gone but isn't.

You don't have to be perfect to have a healthy relationship. You just have to be present. This book is your invitation back—to yourself, to your partner, and to the possibility that love can be rebuilt, stronger than before.

# UNDERSTANDING THE CYCLE

Sue Johnson, the founder of Emotionally Focused Therapy (EFT), once said, "The best way to build a relationship is to understand the patterns that fuel disconnection and have the courage to change them" (Johnson, 2008). That's really what this workbook is all about. It brings together what Amber and I learned in our own healing journey and the research-backed tools of attachment science and couples therapy to help you and your partner slow down, see your patterns more clearly, and begin creating new ways of connecting that feel safe, secure, and lasting.

One of the most common dynamics a couple experiences is what Johnson (2008, 2019) describes as the demand/withdraw—or pursue/withdraw—pattern. We'll use the term "pursue/withdraw" throughout this workbook to describe a dance where one partner, feeling disconnected, reaches for closeness, while the other, feeling overwhelmed or criticized, pulls away. It's not about who's right or wrong—it's about how fear and longing collide. Once you can see that pattern, you can begin to change it.

## Here are a few examples of how that dance might look in real life:

- One partner asks to talk through something difficult, hoping to feel closer, while the other pulls back, trying to prevent a fight.

- One partner shares emotions to process and feel reassured, while the other turns inward, trying to stay calm and avoid escalation.

- One partner pushes for resolution quickly, not wanting conflict to linger, while the other withdraws, needing space to think.

- One partner raises their voice to be heard, while the other grows quiet, hoping to protect the relationship from more pain.

Each partner's behavior in the pursue/withdraw cycle is a strategy—an attempt to manage distress and preserve connection (Johnson, 2008). The pursuer often longs for closeness and reassurance, while the withdrawer is often trying to prevent conflict or emotional over-whelm. Neither partner is the problem. The real issue is the cycle itself—the patterned dance of protest and retreat that unintentionally keeps both people from feeling safe and seen. When we understand that each position is rooted in protection and attachment needs, we move from blame to compassion, and from disconnection to healing.

Over time, this dynamic can create emotional distance, frustration, and unmet needs. The more one partner pushes for connection, the more the other withdraws—leaving both exhausted and misunder-stood (Johnson, 2019).

That's why I created this 90-day journey: to help couples see their cycle, slow it down, and create safer, more connected ways of relat-ing. In my years of practice, I've seen the pursue/withdraw pattern show up in nearly every couple. It's common. It's painful. But it's also highly treatable. With insight, intention, and practice, the very pattern that once divided you can become your path to deeper con-nection.

## Breaking the Cycle

Let's explore five research-informed steps to help you recognize, interrupt, and begin reshaping your negative cycle. These steps are grounded in the work of Sue Johnson's *Emotionally Focused Ther-apy* (Johnson, 2008, 2019) and John and Julie Gottman's research on healthy communication (Gottman & Silver, 1999; Gottman & Gottman, 2017).

1. **Regulate Before You Relate**
   When emotions run high, your nervous system may shift into fight, flight, freeze, or fawn. Take a moment to pause and breathe. This gives your body a chance to settle and allows you to engage your partner from a more connected state. Gottman calls this *physiological self-soothing* (Gottman & Silver, 1999).

   Try this: Place a hand on your heart, take three slow breaths, and say silently: "We're on the same team."

2. **Name the Pattern, Not the Person**

   Johnson (2008) teaches that the cycle—not your partner—is the real enemy. When you notice your familiar dance begin (blame, retreat, pursue, shut down), pause and say together: "This feels like our pattern. Let's hit pause before it goes further."

   Naming the cycle externalizes the problem and invites teamwork, not blame.

3. **Share What's Underneath**

   Instead of rehashing old fights or defending yourself, take a moment to share what's really happening inside—your fear, longing, or hurt. That's what EFT calls *primary emotion* (Johnson, 2019).

   "I'm not mad—I'm just feeling disconnected and unsure if I matter to you right now."

4. **Attune and Validate**

   Rather than fixing or debating, offer *attunement*—the active, ongoing effort to "feel felt" by one another (Siegel, 2010). It's the practice of sensing, understanding, and responding to each other's emotional signals accurately enough that both partners feel seen, safe, and connected.

   "That makes sense why you'd feel that way. I didn't realize it landed like that."

   Validation doesn't mean agreement—it means your partner's emotional world matters to you (Gottman & Gottman, 2017).

5. **Use "I" Statements with Structure**

   Slow down the conversation by taking turns and using "I" statements to express your feelings and needs clearly. Gottman & Gottman (2017) emphasize this as a key repair tool.

   Examples:

   - "I feel overwhelmed when we argue late at night—I need time earlier in the day to process things better."
   - "I feel alone when we don't check in. I need to feel like we're still on the same team."

It may feel awkward at first. But uncommon connection requires uncommon communication.

Disrupting a long-standing pattern isn't easy—but with consistency and curiosity, you can move from disconnection to understanding. These five steps aren't just about communication—they're about creating emotional safety, which is the foundation of secure connection.

*Uncommon connection requires uncommon communication.*

## Repair

Healing is simple, but it's not easy. Why? Real life is messy. Emotions get intense. We all hit a boiling point. It's natural to want to quit or give up when things get hard. But this workbook is here to give you the tools to keep going, even when it feels tough. You'll learn how to slow down the emotions and disrupt the negative cycles that have kept you stuck.

One of the most powerful predictors of a healthy relationship isn't the absence of conflict—it's how well couples repair after conflict. According to relationship researcher John Gottman, "Successful couples are able to repair effectively after a fight, and that's what makes the difference" (Gottman & Silver, 1999). *Repair attempts* are the efforts partners make to de-escalate tension, soothe one another, and reconnect emotionally. Whether it's a gentle touch, a kind word, or a humorous comment, these moments signal a desire to return to safety and understanding. When these repair attempts are received with openness rather than defensiveness, healing begins. In fact, it's not the absence of rupture that defines strong couples—it's the presence of meaningful repair (Gottman & Gottman, 2017).

This workbook was designed with that very purpose in mind: to create intentional opportunities for corrective experiences. As you move through these 90 days together, you'll be invited into small but significant moments of emotional honesty, reflection, and reconnection. Each prompt, exercise, and conversation is a doorway to greater intimacy and healing. Whether you're rebuilding trust, recovering from disconnection, or simply trying to grow deeper, this workbook helps you slow down your negative cycle and establish a rhythm of repair. When practiced consistently, these moments become a new kind of muscle memory—one where safety, curiosity, and compassion replace old patterns of blame, withdrawal, or escalation.

## A Journey Worth Taking

*Secure* is written for couples who feel like they're drifting and need a way back to one another—or for those who simply want to strengthen the relationship they already have. It's for partners who are ready to grow, heal, and reconnect—not by avoiding the hard stuff, but by gently leaning in. Whether your relationship feels distant or steady, this workbook offers a daily path toward deeper connection, emotional safety, and lasting closeness.

If you're holding this book, it likely means that you and your partner are committed to facing the challenges that naturally arise in any relationship—not as adversaries, but as teammates. Every relationship has its own story, shaped by unique experiences, past wounds, and learned patterns. While it's easy to point fingers or assign blame, true growth begins when both partners acknowledge their own work to do. The good news? You don't have to do it alone.

This 90-day (or 13-week) journey isn't about perfection—it's about progress. The work ahead will be transformative, but it will also take real commitment from both of you. Like anything meaningful in life, building a relationship where you both feel seen, valued, and loved requires time, energy, and intentionality. There will be days when the work feels easy and hopeful, and others when it stirs up frustration, discomfort, or old pain. That's not failure—that's healing. Growth often arrives disguised as discomfort, inviting us to face the parts of ourselves and our relationship that we've avoided. But those moments, as hard as they are, are also where real repair begins.

*Growth often arrives disguised as discomfort.*

This work is about choosing each other again and again, especially when it would be easier to pull away. Some days will stretch you, but if you stay honest, curious, and open, you'll come out stronger, more connected, and more secure. Over time, you'll build a foundation of trust, intimacy, and mutual respect that can weather anything life brings your way.

If you're willing to show up, stay present, and do the work—even on the days you'd rather shut down—you'll begin to see the shift. It won't happen overnight, and it won't always be neat, but it will be real. Couples who lean into this kind of intentional growth report greater satisfaction, stronger emotional bonds, and a deeper understanding of themselves and each other (Gottman & Gottman, 2017; Johnson, 2019). This isn't maintenance—it's an investment. And like any worthwhile investment, it takes patience, grace, and grit.

But don't let that intimidate you. The process is also filled with beauty—moments of laughter you didn't expect, glimpses of your partner that catch you off guard in the best way, and small wins that remind you why you're doing this. You'll rediscover what drew you together in the first place. You'll learn things about each other that surprise you, soften you, and heal you. It's hard. It's holy. And it's worth every step.

To do this kind of work well, it helps to carry these four qualities along the way:

1. **Determination** – to keep showing up, even when it's hard.
2. **Consistency** – because lasting change comes from daily effort.
3. **Openness** – to see yourself and your partner with fresh eyes.
4. **Vulnerability** – to let love grow in the places that once felt too tender to touch.

The work ahead will require all four—but your relationship is worth it. You've chosen to share your life with one person; what if you could make the most of it by committing to the hard work of healing, connecting, and growing together? That's why this workbook exists. The tools inside are the same ones that helped our marriage heal over a decade ago.

REPS is the rhythm of this workbook — a simple but powerful model designed to help you grow emotional connection through practice.

Like building physical strength, relational strength comes from repetition. The more REPS you put in, the stronger your bond becomes.

## R — Reflect

Slow down. Notice what's happening inside you before reacting. Reflection builds self-awareness — the foundation for connection. You can't share what you don't yet understand.

Ask yourself:

- What am I really feeling right now?
- What story am I telling myself?
- What do I most need?

## E — Engage

Engage is where reflection turns into connection. It's your invitation to move — to write, notice, or talk together. Some days you'll jot down thoughts; other days you'll lean in through conversation or simple presence.

## P — Prompt

Prompts give you language for vulnerability. They help you move beyond surface talk into real emotional honesty. Most start with "I" statements or open questions.

Examples:

- "I feel _____ because _____."
- "What I really need right now is _____."

## S — Share

This is where connection deepens. Sharing invites your partner into your emotional world — not to fix you, but to *know* you.

Example: *"When you asked if I was okay earlier, I said yes — but I actually felt hurt and didn't know how to say it."*

## Why It Works

**REPS** mirrors what research shows about emotionally healthy relationships: safety and closeness grow through consistent, intentional communication. **Spending 20-30 minutes a day** with each **REPS** will help rewire your relationship toward empathy, understanding, and secure love.

## RelationTips

Throughout this workbook, you'll notice short insights called RelationTips. These are bite-sized reflections, reminders, or truths designed to help you pause, breathe, and refocus on what matters most—connection.

Think of a RelationTip as a small spark of encouragement or wisdom that keeps you grounded in the "why" behind the work. Some will challenge your thinking. Others will affirm what you're learning. All of them are crafted to help you integrate new habits of love, empathy, and emotional safety into your daily life.

Each RelationTip reflects research-backed truths from attachment science, communication theory, and emotional intelligence—but written in a way that feels personal and practical. These brief reminders will help you:

- Reframe your perspective when conflict arises.
- Remember your tools when stress makes you forget.
- Reignite your hope when growth feels slow.

Example:
RelationTip: You only get out of this work what you put into this work.

## Research-Based Tools and Personal Experience

This 90-day workbook is shaped by a blend of personal experience and several research-backed approaches to relationship health. While Sue Johnson's Emotionally Focused Therapy (EFT) and the Gottman Method are the two most frequently used frameworks throughout this workbook, they're not the only ones. You'll also notice threads of attachment science, polyvagal theory, and experiential therapy—woven together with practical tools and honest insights from our own marriage journey. These methods are not just theory. They've been tested in clinical settings and lived out in real relationships—including our own.

## Consistency is Key

According to research by Phillippa Lally and her colleagues at University College London, it takes an average of 66 days to form a new habit—showing that lasting change doesn't happen overnight but through steady, repeated action over time (Lally, van Jaarsveld, Potts, & Wardle, 2010). This finding reminds us that transformation—whether in personal growth or relationships—is not about willpower or quick fixes. It's about consistency.

Psychologist Wendy Wood expands on this idea, noting that habits are built through repetition and environmental support, not just motivation. In her research on behavioral change, she found that consistent patterns of action—especially small, repeatable ones—are what sustain long-term success (Wood, 2019). The brain actually learns stability through rhythm, predictability, and reinforcement. This is as true for our emotional lives as it is for our daily routines.

In relationships, consistency is more than routine—it's the daily decision to show up for your partner, even in the smallest ways. Each act of kindness, each moment of patience, and every attempt at repair communicates, "You can count on me." Over time, these micro-moments create a sense of safety and trust that becomes the foundation of emotional security.

That's why *Secure* is built around a 90-day (13-week) framework: enough time for repetition to become rhythm. These three months are not about checking boxes—they're about building sustainable habits of connection, understanding, and repair. As you move through this journey, remember that progress often happens quietly, through consistent, intentional choices that slowly reshape the heart of your relationship.

## Tips for Maximizing This Journey

- **Individual Copies:** It's best if each partner has their own workbook for personal reflection, but if you prefer to share, one copy can still work just fine.

- **Pacing Options:** Complete this workbook in 90 days or over 13 weeks. For example, if doing 90 days isn't possible, choose the first day of each week as your focus. That will give you 13 weeks of exercises—but we encourage all 90 days to maximize your experience.

- **Writing & Reflection:** Journaling or voice memos are encouraged to track your progress and insights.

- **Flexibility:** If you miss a day, restart without pressure. Progress, not perfection, is the goal.

- **Terminology:** Terms like *partnership, marriage,* and *relationship* are used interchangeably to include anyone in a committed relationship.

Each page of this workbook is an invitation—to pause, reflect, and take one small step closer to one another. Some days will feel light and encouraging; others may stir something deeper. Both matter. Every reflection, every honest word, every shared moment adds to the rhythm of growth you're creating together.

You don't have to rush or get it perfect. Just keep showing up— with curiosity, kindness, and a willingness to see and be seen. That's where change begins.

So take a breath. You're not behind; you're right on time. You've chosen to invest in love—the kind that lasts.

Let's begin.

# WEEK 1

# WHERE LOVE
# FEELS SAFE

# Week 1: Where Love Feels Safe

## Emotional Safety

Can you imagine a relationship where love feels safe—most of the time? Not perfect, not conflict-free, but a space where you both feel secure enough to be real, honest, and seen. No relationship feels emotionally safe 100% of the time—we're all just messy humans doing our best to love well. But what if, over these next 90 days, you could foster more safety, calm, and connection in your relationship?

Emotional safety is the deep sense of security that allows us to be open, honest, and vulnerable without fear of judgment, rejection, or harm. It's what gives us the courage to bring our full selves into the relationship—the beautiful, the broken, and everything in between.

Sue Johnson reminds us that emotional safety is the foundation of any relationship. Without it, we cannot be our best selves with each other. We need emotional safety to be open, honest, and vulnerable with our partner (Johnson, 2008). When emotional safety is present, both partners feel accepted, understood, and supported. It becomes possible to speak freely, repair conflict, and grow together.

Over the next seven days, we'll explore what safety looks like, how it's built, and how to notice when it slips. The goal isn't to create perfection—it's to build a kind of security you can return to when life feels unsteady.

## Our Journey Toward Emotional Safety

For many years, emotional safety wasn't something Amber and I really understood. We didn't know what it looked like, much less how to build it. We had to learn it the hard way—through pain, therapy, and time. But what we discovered changed everything.

We realized that emotional safety doesn't mean avoiding conflict or pretending everything is okay. It means creating a space where both people can be fully seen, fully known, and still fully loved. That kind of safety takes courage, patience, and daily practice.

As we learned, the road to emotional safety isn't paved with comfort—it's paved with vulnerability.

## The Paradox of Vulnerability

Here's one of the great ironies of love: the very thing we need to feel safe—connection—requires us to do the thing that feels the most unsafe—be vulnerable.

Vulnerability asks us to take off our armor, to show what's real, even when it's uncomfortable. It's risky, yes, but it's also the only path to deep, lasting trust.

At its core, vulnerability is about being seen. And being seen—fully, without pretense—is terrifying when we've been taught to protect ourselves from rejection, judgment, or abandonment.

Many of us have learned, through past relationships, childhood wounds, or cultural messages, that revealing too much is dangerous. Maybe in your childhood, emotions were dismissed. You were told to "stop crying" or "toughen up," so vulnerability became something to suppress. Maybe in past relationships, your openness was met with criticism. You shared something personal, only to have it used against you later. Maybe you were hurt by people who should have protected you. And now, your nervous system treats vulnerability as a threat.

These experiences train us to armor up. We become guarded, careful with our words, hesitant to share our deeper feelings. The problem is that the very armor we use to protect ourselves also keeps us from experiencing the closeness we crave.

The moments you choose to stay open instead of shutting down are what build safety. Vulnerability may feel like exposure, but it's actually the birthplace of trust.

# Markers of Emotional Safety

As a therapist, I see how crucial emotional safety is for every couple I work with. Without it, partners either walk on eggshells or shut down completely. So, what does emotional safety look like in real life? Here are five markers that help you recognize when it's present—and when it's missing.

1. **Consistency and Reliability: "I Can Count on You."**
   Emotional safety is built on knowing your partner will show up for you—physically and emotionally—when you need them. Reliability strengthens trust.

   *Example:* After a long, stressful day, you vent to your partner about work. Instead of brushing you off, they respond, "That sounds overwhelming. Do you want to talk about it, or do you just need me to listen?"

   *Unsafe Dynamic:* Your partner dismisses your feelings, saying, "Ugh, you always stress about work. Just let it go."

2. **Freedom to Express Thoughts and Feelings: "I Can Be Myself."**

   A safe relationship allows both partners to share their inner world—fears, dreams, concerns—without fearing judgment or ridicule.

   *Example:* You tell your partner that you've been feeling disconnected lately. Instead of getting defensive, they say, "I don't want you to feel that way. Let's talk about how we can reconnect."

   *Unsafe Dynamic:* Your partner responds with, "Oh, so now I'm not enough for you? Maybe you're the one being distant."

3. **Ability to Handle Conflict Without Fear: "I Can Disagree Without It Leading to Disaster."**

   Conflict is inevitable, but emotionally safe couples know that disagreement doesn't mean disconnection.

   *Example:* You and your partner argue about finances. Instead of shutting down or escalating, they say, "I know money is a stress point for both of us. Let's figure out a plan together."

*Unsafe Dynamic:* Your partner lashes out, "You're impossible to talk to! Maybe I should just handle the money since you can't!"

4. **Mutual Respect for Boundaries: "My Needs and Limits Matter."**

Partners in an emotionally safe relationship honor each other's boundaries—not as obstacles, but as expressions of love.

*Example:* You express that you need time to decompress after work. Your partner responds, "Got it, take your time. I'll be here when you're ready to talk."

*Unsafe Dynamic:* Your partner makes you feel guilty, "Wow, so now you don't even want to spend time with me? Cool."

5. **A Culture of Repair: "We Make Things Right When We Mess Up."**

No relationship is perfect, but emotionally safe couples repair quickly when they hurt each other.

*Example:* Your partner snaps at you in frustration, then later says, "I was harsh, and that wasn't fair to you. I'm sorry—can we talk about what happened?"

*Unsafe Dynamic:* Instead of owning their mistake, they say, "Well, if you hadn't annoyed me, I wouldn't have snapped."

These markers don't describe a perfect relationship; they describe a *growing* one. Each moment of repair, empathy, or understanding becomes a small act of safety-building.

## The Courage to Step In

There's no shortcut to emotional safety. You build it slowly, one honest moment at a time—by risking vulnerability and proving, through experience, that it's safe to be fully seen. The road may feel shaky at first, especially if trust has been tested or distance has crept in. But every small act of openness—every repaired misunderstanding, every gentle truth spoken—becomes a brick in the foundation of a secure love.

Stepping into this work takes courage. It means choosing curiosity over comfort, truth over pretense, and connection over self-protection. It means remembering that love isn't built on perfection, but on presence—the willingness to keep showing up even when it feels uncertain.

This week, your only job is to notice—notice when safety grows, when it falters, and what helps restore it. You're not fixing your relationship; you're learning to feel safe enough to grow inside it.

What's on the other side of that courage is something beautiful: a love that feels calm, steady, and safe enough to grow. A love that welcomes the whole of who you are.

So before we begin, take a deep breath. You've already done the hardest part—you've decided to show up.

Now, let's begin the work of building emotional safety—or strengthening the foundation you already share.

# Day 1: Recognizing Emotional Safety

Before diving into the deeper work, today is about noticing what's already working. Every couple has places—big or small—where emotional safety exists. Naming those moments helps us build from strength, not just from struggle.

## Reflect

Since we're starting with exploring emotional safety, take a few minutes to think about the ways you already feel safe in your relationship.

Examples:

- "I can tell my partner anything—my fears, my dreams, even the things I'm ashamed of—without worrying they'll judge me."
- "When we argue, I know we'll still be okay. I don't have to fear being shut out or punished."
- "I feel seen, valued, and loved for who I truly am—not just for what I do."

## Engage

Write down three specific behaviors or actions from your partner that help you feel emotionally safe.

1. _____

2. _____

3. _____

## Prompt

Ask your partner: "Can I share some things that make me feel safe with you? I want you to know how much these things mean to me."

## Share

Take turns sharing the three specific behaviors you wrote. Notice how it feels to hear these affirmations—and how it feels to say them out loud. Once you have both shared, there's nothing else to do for today. Just allow the positive words spoken to settle into your heart.

**RelationTip:** Start slow. Today isn't about fixing anything—it's about noticing what's already safe. Safety grows from the small, steady moments that say, "I'm here, and I'm not going anywhere"

# Day 2: Creating Supportive Space

"As partners, it is our responsibility to create a safe and supportive environment where we can each feel emotionally secure. This means taking personal responsibility for our own emotional well-being and being mindful of how our words and actions impact our partner." (Johnson, 2019)

Yesterday, we began by exploring emotional safety. Today, we are going to deepen the reach for emotional safety through personal responsibility. Emotional safety isn't just created by our partner—it's cultivated by how we each show up. When both people take ownership of their words, tone, and behavior, the relationship begins to feel more grounded, calm, and trustworthy (Tatkin, 2012).

## Reflect

Think about ways you and your partner can create a safe emotional space for one another. Emotional safety requires personal responsibility for your own well-being and mindfulness of how your words and actions affect your partner.

## Engage

Write down one specific way you can take personal responsibility for creating emotional safety in your relationship.

_____

_____

_____

## Prompt

"A way I can create emotional safety for you is_____

_____."

## Share

Discuss how you can both put these commitments into action.

**RelationTip:** Emotional safety isn't something you wait for—it's something you build by showing up with intention, gentleness, and ownership

# Day 3: Attached

Often, we move forward in building safety by first looking back. That's the focus of days three and four.

Every one of us learned about safety and love long before we ever knew the words. We learned it through presence or absence, comfort or silence, consistency or chaos. Those early lessons didn't just teach us how to survive—they taught us how to connect, how to reach for safety, and what to expect when we did.

If emotional safety is the foundation of connection, attachment is the blueprint that shows us how we build it.

So what do I mean by *attachment*?
Attachment is the emotional bond that forms between two people—a connection that shapes how we seek closeness, handle distance, and respond to distress. From infancy, this bond teaches us what love feels like and how safe it is to depend on someone. Those early experiences become the model we carry into every relationship, including the one we're in now.

The way we give and receive safety today is often a reflection of how we first learned to connect, seek comfort, and handle distress. Before we ever fell in love, we were already being shaped for it.

The safety we experience—or struggle to create—in our relationships isn't random—it's rooted in those earliest attachment experiences. Our nervous systems remember what it felt like to reach out and be met—or not.

From our first cries as infants to the moments we reached for comfort—or learned not to—our attachment experiences laid the groundwork for how we relate to others as adults (Bowlby, 1988; Johnson, 2019). Some of us learned that love feels consistent and safe. Others learned that love can be conditional, unpredictable, or even painful.

These early lessons didn't simply fade with time—they became the wiring that determines how we respond when closeness feels uncertain or when safety is at risk.

Understanding this wiring isn't about blaming the past; it's about bringing compassion and clarity to it. When we see how our attachment story shows up in the present, we can begin to respond instead of react—to move toward our partner with awareness instead of fear. This is how we start creating the emotional safety we've always needed, both for ourselves and for the people we love.

## Why Attachment Matters

Emotional safety and attachment are deeply intertwined. You can't truly build one without understanding the other. Exploring attachment helps us recognize why we protect, pursue, withdraw, or shut down when we feel disconnected. It reveals the hidden patterns that drive our behaviors and gives us language for what we've felt all along.

Understanding attachment is one of the most powerful steps toward breaking unhealthy cycles and creating a relationship where both partners feel truly safe, seen, and loved (Johnson, 2008). From the moment we enter the world, we rely on caregivers to meet our needs—both physical and emotional. Depending on how consistently those needs were met, we developed a way of relating to others that still influences us today (Ainsworth et al., 1978).

## For example:

- When love felt dependable and caregivers were emotionally available, we learned that relationships are safe and trustworthy.

- When care was unpredictable or inconsistent, we learned to cling or question love, fearing it might disappear.

- When emotions were ignored or dismissed, we learned to go quiet, depend on ourselves, and keep others at a distance.

- When love and fear coexisted, we learned that closeness could feel both necessary and dangerous (Main & Solomon, 1990).

These early patterns don't simply fade with time—they continue to influence how we communicate, seek reassurance, and navigate conflict. If we never name them, they quietly run the show. But when we do, we gain a roadmap for change and the tools to create the kind of emotional safety that heals.

Now that you understand how attachment connects to emotional safety, let's look more closely at how these styles show up in real relationships.

## Understanding the Four Attachment Styles

Your attachment style influences how you experience emotional safety, express needs, and handle conflict. Below are the four primary attachment styles and how they typically appear in relationships (Johnson, 2019; Tatkin, 2012).

1. **Secure Attachment – "I Trust You and I Trust Myself."**

   A securely attached person feels comfortable with both intimacy and independence. They believe relationships are safe, conflict can be resolved, and love is dependable.

   Markers of secure attachment include the ability to express needs openly, trust your partner to respond with care, and repair ruptures quickly (Johnson, 2008; Tatkin, 2012).

   **Examples:**
   "I'm feeling overwhelmed right now, but I know we can figure this out together."
   "I need a little time to think, but I'm not going anywhere."
   "That hurt when you said that—can we talk about what's going on between us?"

   When emotional safety is missing, a securely attached partner may begin to doubt their partner's love—not because of their partner's actions, but because conflict triggers old insecurities.

2. **Anxious / Preoccupied (Ambivalent) Attachment – "Do You Still Love Me?"**

People with an anxious attachment style crave closeness but often fear rejection or abandonment. They may become preoccupied with their partner's responses and need frequent reassurance (Ainsworth et al., 1978; Johnson, 2008).

Markers include worry about a partner's feelings, overanalyzing behaviors, and difficulty self-soothing.

**Examples:**
"Are you mad at me? You feel really far away right now."
"Why won't you just talk to me? I hate not knowing where we stand."
"I feel like I'm the only one fighting for us—do you even care?"

When emotional safety is missing, distance feels like danger, leading to clinginess or withdrawal driven by fear of rejection.

3. **Avoidant / Dismissive Attachment – "I Don't Want to Need Anyone."**

People with an avoidant attachment style value independence and may struggle with emotional closeness. They often pull away when relationships feel too intense or when emotions become overwhelming (Shaver & Mikulincer, 2002).

Markers include discomfort with dependence, preference for logic over emotion, and minimizing emotional needs (Tatkin, 2012).

**Examples:**
"Can we just drop it? Talking about this makes it worse."
"I'm fine. I just need some space to think."
"You're overreacting—it's not that big of a deal."

When emotional safety is missing, avoidant partners may withdraw completely, avoiding the conversation or minimizing their partner's concerns.

4. **Disorganized / Fearful-Avoidant Attachment – "I Want You Close, But I'm Scared."**

A person with disorganized attachment often experiences both a deep desire for connection and an equally strong fear of it. This style is often rooted in early experiences where caregivers were both a source of comfort and fear (Main & Solomon, 1990)

Markers include emotional reactivity, alternating between craving closeness and pushing a partner away, and fearing abandonment while feeling overwhelmed by intimacy.

**Examples:**
"I want to talk, but I'm afraid you'll just shut me down."
"Part of me wants to be close to you, and part of me just wants to run."
"Every time I try to open up, I feel like I'll get hurt again."

When emotional safety is missing, partners with this style can become caught in a push-pull cycle that leaves both people feeling drained and uncertain.

Understanding your attachment style isn't about labeling yourself or your partner—it's about recognizing the patterns that shape how you give and receive love. Awareness brings compassion; compassion opens the door to change.

## How Attachment Insecurity Sparks the Cycle

Once you begin identifying your style, you'll start to see how different attachment pairings create predictable patterns—what Sue Johnson calls *the dance* or *the negative cycle*.

- If you lean **Anxious** and your partner leans **Avoidant**: Their pause or space can feel like rejection, even though it's meant to calm the heat.

  **Reframe:** "Their stepping back is a soothing strategy, not proof I'm unlovable."

- If you lean **Avoidant** and your partner leans **Anxious**: Their bids for closeness may feel like scrutiny or control, but they're attempts to reconnect.

  **Reframe:** "Their reaching is a safety signal, not an attack."

- If you lean **Fearful-Avoidant** and your partner is **Anxious**: Your mixed signals amplify their alarm about being left.

**Reframe:** "My toggling is my body's old alarm, not today's truth."

- If you lean **Fearful-Avoidant** and your partner is **Avoidant**: Distance feels safe until it turns into loneliness.

  **Reframe:** "We're both protecting the bond by staying cool—let's name needs gently and early."

- If one partner is **Secure**: Their calm may be misread as indifference or intrusion.

  **Reframe:** "Their calm face is a bridge, not a shutdown or takeover."

**Bottom line:** Each partner's move is a strategy to manage distress and protect the bond. The cycle—not either person—is the opponent (Johnson, 2008).

## The Connection Between Attachment and Emotional Safety

Emotional safety in a relationship can feel natural or foreign, depending on our attachment history. If you've always known safe connection, feeling secure with your partner may come easily. But if emotional safety wasn't modeled for you as a child, it may feel uncomfortable—or even impossible—to trust that someone will truly stay, listen, or love you at your most vulnerable moments (Bowlby, 1988).

Exploring attachment isn't about blame—it's about awareness. Without it, we risk misinterpreting our partner's actions and reacting from old wounds, reinforcing cycles that keep emotional safety out of reach.

The good news: attachment insecurity is not a life sentence. It can be healed, and security can be cultivated (Johnson, 2019; Tatkin, 2012). No matter what attachment adaptations you learned early in life, your relationship today can become a space where emotional safety grows. Together, you can co-create a secure, stable bond by learning to communicate, repair ruptures, and meet one another's needs in ways that foster trust, reassurance, and intimacy.

## Call to Action: Watch & Reflect

To dive deeper into this, try these two steps:

1. **Take a free attachment quiz** from The Attachment Project:

2. **Watch this brief video on attachment and love:**

These resources will help you:

- ✓ Identify your attachment style
- ✓ Recognize how attachment impacts your relationship dynamics
- ✓ Learn practical ways to create more emotional safety

After engaging with these, take a few moments to reflect:

- What stood out to you the most?
- Do you see patterns in your own relationship that align with your attachment style?
- What's one small shift you can make today to foster greater emotional safety?

From the video, which attachment style resonated with you?

_____

## Reflect

Think about your childhood and how your caregivers impacted your view of relationships.

## Engage

Jot down how this might affect your relationship today: _____

_____

_____

_____

## Prompt

"I think my relationship with _____ (mom, dad, grandparent, adoptive caregiver, etc.) shaped how I view _____ (love, trust, emotions), and I see it in our relationship when I _____."

## Share

After sharing, access empathy by affirming your partner with:

"That all makes sense. I'm so sorry you had that experience. Thank you for sharing that with me. Is there anything I can do to support you with that?"

Or, if your partner had a more secure experience:

"I'm so glad you had that kind of stability growing up. I want us to have that same sense of security together."

**RelationTip:** This is a time for connection, not for fixing or analyzing. Simply hold space for your partner's experience.

# Day 4: Attachment in the Moment

Yesterday you mapped the attachment style/story. Today you'll use it. When tension rises, attachment patterns show up fast—often in the body before the brain. If Day 3 explained the *map*, Day 4 is about *navigation*: noticing your early signals, naming your protect/ protest move, and choosing a safer next step together.

## Spot your protect/protest move

When connection feels uncertain, most of us do one of three things to feel safer:

- **Protest (pursue):** press, question, repeat yourself, get loud or urgent to pull closeness back.
- **Protect (pull back):** get quiet, logical, change the subject, or disappear to cool things down.
- **Toggle (mixed):** reach in, then retreat; say "come close" and "not too close" in the same moment.

None of these makes you the villain. They're old safety strategies. Naming them gives you choice.

## A 3-step pause you can use today

1. **Notice (body cue):** "My chest got tight… jaw clenched… eyes averted."
2. **Name (soft feeling + story):** "Underneath I feel sad/scared; the story says, 'I'm losing you.'"
3. **Ask (clear, doable need):** "Could you sit with me and hold my hand for a minute?" or "Can we take 90 seconds and then try again?"

## Reflect

Think of a recent moment when things felt off between you. What happened in your *body* first? What protect/protest move did you reach for?

## Engage

Complete these quick lines (write, don't overthink):

- "When _____ happens, my body does _____."
- "My default move is to _____ (protest/protect/toggle)."
- "Underneath, the softer feeling is _____ and the story says _____."
- "A small thing that helps me feel safer is _____ (specific, doable)."

## Prompt

"When _____ happens, I feel (primary emotion) and I tend to _____ (my protect/protest move). Underneath I'm needing _____. In this moment, it would help if you could _____."

## Share

Trade your prompts. Listen without fixing. Then agree on one **reset ritual** you'll try for the next week when either of you notices the pattern (examples: a hand squeeze + the word "team," a 90-second pause with a return time, three slow breaths while making eye contact).

**RelationTip:** Name the *move*, not the *person*. Treat the cycle as the opponent and each other as allies. The moment you can say "there's our pattern" together, you're already safer. (Johnson 2008)

# Day 5: Repairing Safety After Rupture

Yesterday you learned how to notice what happens *inside you* when safety feels uncertain. Today, you'll learn how to name what happens *between you* when safety has been disrupted.

Every couple experiences moments of rupture—times when trust, understanding, or connection breaks down. Maybe it's a harsh tone, a moment of defensiveness, or an unmet bid for comfort. These moments can stir old attachment wounds and make love feel risky again.

But here's the good news: emotional safety isn't about avoiding rupture—it's about how you repair it. When you share your experience with honesty and empathy, you teach each other that safety can be rebuilt, even after hurt (Johnson, 2008).

## Reflect

Think back to a moment in your relationship when you felt emotionally unsafe or disconnected. What was happening inside you in that moment? What did you need most that you didn't receive?

## Engage

Take a few minutes to write about what this moment meant to you—not to analyze or assign blame, but to understand what the experience touched in you.

"When _____ happened, I felt _____ because _____."

"What I needed in that moment was _____."

## Prompt

"I want to share something that still feels tender for me—not because I want to revisit the conflict, but because I want us to understand each other more deeply. When _____ happened, I felt _____. What I really needed was _____."

## Share

Take turns sharing. As you listen, focus on empathy, not defense. Try saying:

- "That makes sense. I can see why that felt unsafe."
- "I didn't realize that landed that way. Thank you for trusting me with it."
- "What can I do differently next time to help you feel safe?"

Then, simply sit in quiet connection for a moment. Let understanding do its work.

**RelationTip:** Safety isn't the absence of conflict—it's the confidence that you'll come back to each other afterward. Repair is where real trust is born.

# Day 6: Emotional Triggers

Yesterday, you explored what happens when safety feels uncertain. Today, we'll look at the moments that *set those patterns in motion*—the emotional triggers that pull us away from connection before we even realize it.

Emotional triggers threaten safety by sparking fast, automatic reactions that lead to misunderstanding or distance. When a trigger is activated, it often touches an old fear: being rejected, controlled, abandoned, or not enough. The reaction may look like anger, withdrawal, criticism, or silence—but underneath, it's usually fear.

Learning to identify and name your triggers helps you slow the cycle before it gains momentum. When you notice your reaction rising, pause and ask:

"What is this really touching in me? What do I need right now to feel safe again?"

Below is a list of common relational triggers. Highlight those that feel familiar or add your own. (Bowlby, 1988; Tatkin, 2012; Johnson, 2019)

## Connection-Related Triggers
- Feeling ignored, dismissed, or unseen.
- Emotional distance or lack of responsiveness.
- Silence, withdrawal, or avoidance during conflict.
- Lack of affection, reassurance, or quality time.
- Partner seeming preoccupied or unavailable.

## Autonomy-Related Triggers
- Feeling pressured to open up or talk when not ready.

- Partner pushing for resolution before you've cooled down.
- Losing personal space, time, or boundaries.
- Feeling controlled, criticized, or "talked over."
- Partner's strong emotions feeling overwhelming or intrusive.

## Worthiness-Related Triggers

- Feeling unappreciated, unimportant, or "not enough."
- Receiving criticism, correction, or comparison.
- Feeling blamed or misunderstood.
- Sensing disappointment or disapproval from your partner.

## Safety-Related Triggers

- Fear of abandonment, rejection, or being left alone.
- Conflict escalating quickly or voices rising.
- Partner appearing angry, detached, or unpredictable.
- Old memories of being shamed or ignored resurfacing.

## Reflect

Bring to mind a few moments that tend to activate you. What pattern do you notice? Do your triggers center more around *disconnection, pressure, criticism,* or *loss of control?*

## Engage

Write down three of your common triggers and how they impact your relationship.

1. _____

2. _____

3. _____

## Prompt

"When I feel triggered, I usually respond by _____

_____. Underneath that,

I'm often feeling _____ and needing

_____."

## Share

Talk with your partner about what happens underneath the trigger. Examples:

- "When you walked away during our argument, I raised my voice—but underneath, I was afraid I didn't matter."
- "When you criticized how I handled it, I shut down—but really I felt shame and wanted reassurance."
- "When you seemed distant last night, I kept asking questions—but really I just felt lonely."

**RelationTip:** Every trigger points to a need—usually for safety, belonging, or respect. When you can name the fear underneath and share it gently, your reactivity becomes a doorway back to connection rather than a wall that divides you. (Johnson, 2019)

# Day 7: Reflecting on Progress

This first week has been about awareness—learning your attachment patterns, naming what feels unsafe, and beginning to recognize the moments when fear or disconnection show up between you. Awareness is always the first step toward change, because you can't heal what you can't see.

As you look back, don't just notice what was hard, notice what *moved.* Maybe you reached for each other instead of retreating. Maybe you softened a reaction or simply stayed present when it would've been easier to shut down. These are small but sacred shifts. Growth often happens quietly, in the pauses, in the gentle words, in the decision to stay curious when it would've been easier to defend (Johnson, 2019).

You've started the work of creating emotional safety—of proving to one another, moment by moment, that it's safe to be real, to be seen, and to be loved there.

## Reflect

Look back on the week's work. Did you notice any patterns or triggers that surfaced? What was easy to talk about, and what was difficult? Did learning about your attachment help you make sense of your inner world?

## Engage

Write down or record a voice memo of any significant insights from this week's work.

_____

_____

_____

## Prompt

"A significant moment for me this week was when I learned _____
_____ about myself."

## Share

Take time to discuss any moments of tension or growth, paying special attention to your attachment style/needs and your emotional triggers. What did you learn about yourself and each other as you reflected on those moments?

**RelationTip:** Emotional safety isn't built in grand moments—it's built in the quiet ones, when you notice your triggers, stay curious, and choose connection instead of protection. Each moment of awareness is a small act of healing (Johnson, 2008).

> _"Being married is like having a best friend who doesn't remember anything you say."_
> **— Anonymous**

# WEEK 2

# THE SPACE
# BETWEEN WORDS

# Week 2: The Space Between Words

*"When someone really hears you without passing judgment on you, without taking responsibility for you, without trying to mold you, it feels damn good."*
**— Carl Rogers (1961, p. 55)**

There's a space—a sacred pause—between what's spoken and what's heard. In that space, understanding can either bloom or break. Most of the time, disconnection doesn't happen because we stop talking, but because we stop hearing. Between every word is a moment where empathy can enter—or exit—the conversation.

Empathy is what transforms communication from information into connection. It's what turns "You're not listening" into "You see me." Real empathy means tuning into the emotion beneath your partner's words—listening not just to respond, but to understand. When empathy fills the space between you, even hard conversations become places of healing instead of hurt.

Sue Johnson reminds us that "empathy is the heartbeat of emotional safety" (Johnson, 2019, p. 42). It's what allows us to stay open, even in the face of pain. When we listen with empathy, we give our partner the gift of feeling safe enough to be real. It's not about fixing or proving a point. It's about creating a moment where both of you can breathe, connect, and feel seen again.

Empathy, like safety, is something you practice into being. It grows through repetition—the daily choice to slow down, to listen longer than feels comfortable, and to care more about understanding than about being right. The more you practice, the more your nervous systems learn to relax in one another's presence.

This week is about slowing down and listening differently—listening in a way that heals instead of defends. Empathy isn't a skill you master once; it's a posture you return to daily.

Below are five simple but powerful ways to begin practicing empathic listening in your relationship. They're not steps to check off—they're reminders of how love sounds when it slows down enough to hear.

## 5 Ways to Practice Empathic Listening

1. **Recognize Emotional Triggers:** Notice what sparks reactivity for each of you. A pursuer may feel hurt when ignored; a withdrawer may feel unsafe in conflict. Awareness helps you both respond with compassion instead of defense (Johnson, 2008).

2. **Give Full Attention:** Put the phone down, make eye contact, and be fully present. Attention is an act of love (Goleman, 1995).

3. **Listen Without Interrupting:** Let your partner finish before responding. You don't have to fix what they're feeling—just hear it.

4. **Reflect What You Hear:** Try saying, "What I'm hearing is that you're feeling _____ because _____. Did I get that right?" Reflection creates emotional safety (Brown, 2012).

5. **Acknowledge Their Feelings:** Validation builds connection. "That makes sense," or "I can see why that would feel hard," can change the emotional temperature in seconds (Gottman & Gottman, 2017).

This week is about slowing down, softening your defenses, and learning to fill the space between words with empathy. When you listen this way, you create more than understanding—you create safety.

# Day 8: Feeling Heard

Before you begin today's exercise, remove distractions, face each other, and agree on one simple job — *"I'm here to understand, not fix."*

> *"Empathy has no script. There's no right or wrong way to do it. It's simply listening, holding space, withholding judgment, emotionally connecting, and communicating that incredibly healing message: 'You're not alone.'"*
> **— Brené Brown (2018, p. 92)**

That's exactly what you'll practice today. Empathy doesn't need perfect words or techniques—it just needs presence. When you feel truly heard, something inside you relaxes. Your nervous system settles. The world feels safer. Feeling heard is one of the most powerful experiences of being loved (Coan & Sbarra, 2015).

## Reflect

Think of a time when you felt truly heard by your partner. What words or actions helped you feel that way? What was it about that moment that allowed you to open up?

## Engage

Write down your partner's words or actions that helped you feel heard.

_____

_____

_____

## Prompt

Actively listen to your partner without interrupting or correcting. Just be present.

"A time when I really felt heard was when _____

_____. That made me

feel like you love and care about me."

## Share

Turn to your partner and share what it was like to be heard without interruption or correction. Then switch roles.

**RelationTip:** Slow down, listen to your partner's response, and attune to them. Remember, "Being heard is so close to being loved that for the average person, they are almost indistinguishable" (Nichols, 2009, p. 17). Once you've both shared, give one another a hug or a high-five and just let it be. You don't have to go deep yet—simply celebrate that you both showed up and tried.

# Day 9: Empathy During Conflict

Conflict has a way of pulling us into defensiveness—where we protect, react, and try to win. But what if we paused and chose empathy instead? Empathy doesn't mean agreeing with everything your partner says; it means working to understand their experience, especially when it's different from your own (Johnson, 2008).

When you choose to see through your partner's eyes, even for a moment, you shift the dynamic from opposition to connection. Today is about practicing empathy not after conflict, but in the middle of it (Gottman & Gottman, 2017).

## Reflect

Identify a specific conflict you've had recently—something minor but real. What feelings came up for you? What story did you tell yourself about your partner in that moment?

## Engage

Choose one part of that conflict and practice empathy in real time. Imagine the situation from your partner's perspective.
Ask yourself:

- *What might they have been feeling or needing in that moment?*
- *What could have been happening beneath their words or tone?*

Write down what they might be feeling or needing in that moment:

_____

_____

_____

## Prompt

You share: "I felt _____ when _____."

Or write your own version here:

_____

_____

_____

## Partner's Response

"Thank you for sharing that. Here's what I think I heard you say…" (Reflect what you think you heard.) "What part of that did I get right?" (Allow your partner to clarify what was missed.)

## Share

How did it go? Did it feel awkward or clunky? That's okay. You're learning a new way of connecting and communicating. Keep practicing and use as many REPS as you need to grow more comfortable.

**RelationTip:** What we hear and what was said are often very different. Don't be surprised when your partner looks at you and says, "That's not what I meant." This is normal. Clarify, reflect again, and keep going.

Why are we doing this? To practice *empathetic listening and responding.* When we slow down our thoughts and regulate our emotions, we can truly hear what's being said — not just what our mind is making up. Our bodies often interpret tone or words as danger, triggering fight, flight, or freeze. By staying present and reflective, we keep the conversation safe. To learn more about this, scan

# Day 10: Clarifying Misunderstandings

Even with the best intentions, communication can get tangled. We misunderstand tone, assume motive, or hear through the filter of our fears. Misunderstandings aren't signs of failure—they're invitations to slow down, check meaning, and repair connection (Gottman & Gottman, 2017).

Empathy helps you bridge the gap between what was said and what was heard. When you practice clarifying, you're not trying to win the conversation; you're trying to understand the heart behind it. Every clarification brings you one step closer to trust.

## Reflect

Think back to yesterday's practice. Was there a moment when something your partner said landed differently than they intended? What do you wish they'd understood about what you were feeling or needing?

## Engage

Before revisiting that moment, take a breath together. Clarifying is not about defending—it's about listening. Decide who will speak first and who will listen. The speaker's goal is to express emotion and need clearly. The listener's goal is to understand, not to solve.

When you're ready, move slowly through the following prompts, keeping your tone soft and your body language open.

## Prompt

## Speaker:

"When _____ happened, I felt _____ because _____. What I needed was _____."

Or

"The part that landed hard for me was _____. Underneath that, I was feeling _____ and needing _____."

## Listener:

1. Reflect: "What I hear you saying is that you felt _____ because _____."
2. Check: "Did I get that right? What did I miss?"
3. Validate: "That makes sense. I can see how that would feel _____."

## Share

Switch roles and repeat the exercise. After both have shared, take a moment together to answer:

- "What shared meaning do we now have about what happened?"
- "What agreement or action would help us next time?"

(Example: "If either of us needs a pause, we'll say 'I need a moment,' and circle back when ready.")

**RelationTip:** Clarifying isn't about proving who's right; it's about aligning on what was felt and what is needed. Every time you slow down to repair a misunderstanding, you're teaching each other that safety matters more than being right (Gottman & Gottman, 2017).

Tomorrow, we'll learn how to express emotions clearly and safely through the use of "I" statements—a skill that keeps empathy alive even in tough conversations.

# Day 11: Speaking from "I"

There's a subtle but powerful shift that happens when we speak from *I* instead of *you.*

"You" statements tend to assign blame, putting our partner on the defensive. "I" statements soften the message and invite understanding. When you start with *I feel* or *I need,* you're taking ownership of your emotions instead of making your partner responsible for them (Rosenberg, 2015).

This shift creates safety—because it's difficult for someone to argue with *your* lived experience.

"I" statements help your partner listen with empathy rather than react with defense. They turn confrontation into communication and help you express the deeper need underneath the frustration (Gottman & Gottman, 2017).

Example:
Instead of saying, *"You make me feel angry when you ignore me,"* try, *"I feel angry when I am ignored."*

See the difference? One points a finger. The other opens a heart.

## Reflect

How often do your conversations begin with "you"? Notice your patterns:

- "You always…"
- "You never…"
- "Why do you…"

Now, pause and ask: What am I actually feeling beneath those statements?

## Engage

Choose one or two real moments from this week where you caught yourself saying "you." Gently rewrite them into "I" statements using the prompts below. The goal isn't perfection—it's honesty. Speak from your own emotion and need, not from your partner's behavior.

## Prompt

"I feel/felt _____ when _____."

Or try:

"What I need right now is _____."

## Share

Discuss what it was like to shift your language. Did it feel awkward or freeing? Was it easier for one of you than the other? How did it change the emotional tone between you?

## Expanded Examples: "You" → "I" Translations

- "You leaving dirty dishes in the sink makes me feel overwhelmed."

    → "I feel overwhelmed when dishes pile up in the sink."

- "You changing plans at the last minute makes me feel frustrated."

    → "I get frustrated when plans change at the last minute."

- "You not acknowledging what I do makes me feel unappreciated."

    → "I feel unappreciated when my efforts go unnoticed."

- "You yelling at me makes me feel hurt."

    → "I feel hurt when voices get raised."

- "You being on your phone during our conversations makes me feel ignored."

    → "I feel ignored when the phone takes more attention than I do."

**RelationTip:** Using "I" statements might feel strange at first—and that's okay. You're retraining your brain to lead with ownership and honesty instead of accusation. If you struggle to name feelings, use a core emotions list or wheel to help identify what's really happening inside (Greenberg, 2016).

# Day 12: Supporting Without Giving Advice

When our partner shares something hard, our instinct is often to help—to fix, guide, or offer a solution. It comes from love, but it can accidentally communicate, *"You shouldn't feel that way,"* or *"Let's move on."*

The truth is, most of the time, your partner isn't asking for a solution—they're asking for connection. Empathy, not advice, is what helps people heal (Brown, 2018).

Listening without fixing takes restraint. It's a spiritual act of humility—choosing presence over performance. It's saying, *"I trust you to find your way, and I'll walk beside you while you do"* (Rogers, 1961).

## Reflect

Think about a time when you shared something difficult and received advice you didn't ask for. Did you feel unseen, misunderstood, or pressured to change your feelings?

## Engage

Take two minutes to write about what it felt like to receive unsolicited advice. Try to name the sensations, emotions, or thoughts that arose for you.

_____

_____

_____

## Prompt

Now, take turns with your partner. One of you will share something personal—a worry, frustration, or even a hope. The other's only job is to listen with presence. No advice. No fixing. Just curiosity and care.

After your partner shares, respond only with empathy using one of the stems below:

- "What I hear you saying is _____."
- "That sounds really hard, and I can imagine you might feel _____."
- "Thank you for trusting me with that."

Then switch roles. When both have shared, take a deep breath together before moving on.

## Share

Talk about what the experience was like.

- How did it feel to simply listen without offering advice or a solution?
- How did it feel to be heard without being "helped"?
- What shifted inside you when you realized listening alone was enough?

**RelationTip:** Giving advice only works when it's being asked for—and even then, it might not land. Sometimes advice sounds like control or criticism, even when it's meant as care. So before you offer advice, ask, *"Do you want me to listen, or do you want help finding a solution?"* (Brown, 2018).

If they say "just listen," give them that gift. Presence often heals more than problem-solving ever could.

*Partnership advice is like broccoli at a BBQ –*
*no one's really excited about it.*

# Day 13: When Advice is Welcome

You've spent this week practicing how to listen without fixing. Today, we'll explore the other side—how to offer perspective in a way that keeps empathy alive.

When advice is truly welcome, it should feel like an offering, not an obligation. Advice lands best when it's wrapped in curiosity and humility, not certainty or urgency (Brown, 2018). Sometimes the most healing sentence you can say is, *"Would you like to hear an idea that might help?"*

## Reflect

Think of a time when someone gave you advice that did feel helpful. What made it different? Did they ask permission first? Did they stay gentle and curious?

## Engage

Write down and area where you might want or might be open to support or advice: _____

_____

_____

_____.

## Prompt

Speaker: "One area where I could use support is _____

_____. I'm open to ideas, but please go slow—I may

need time to process."

Listener: "Thank you for trusting me with that. Would it be helpful if I shared a thought, or would you rather I just listen for now?"

## Share

Discuss what it felt like to give or receive advice with consent. Did it change the emotional tone? Did you feel more connected or more pressured? What did you learn about timing and tenderness?

**RelationTip:** Advice given with permission lands like care. Advice given without it lands like control. Always lead with curiosity—*"Would you like my thoughts?"*—and let their answer guide your next move (Rogers, 1961; Gottman & Gottman, 2017).

# Day 14: Reflecting on Empathy

This week has been about filling the space between words with understanding—learning to listen, clarify, and respond with compassion. You've practiced empathy in the middle of conflict, used "I" statements to stay grounded, and learned the power of presence over problem-solving.

Today is for reflection and gratitude—noticing how far you've come in building emotional safety through empathy.

## Reflect

1. How have I shown empathy toward my partner's emotions this week?

2. When was I most proud of how I responded?

3. What still feels challenging when I try to stay empathetic under stress?

## Engage

Write down one or two moments from this week when empathy changed the direction of a conversation or softened your heart toward your partner.

_____

_____

_____

## Prompt

"One thing I'm taking away from this week is _____

_____."

## Share

Take a few minutes to express appreciation to your partner for showing up, listening, and practicing empathy with you this week. Let them know what it has meant to feel heard and safe.

**RelationTip:** Empathy doesn't mean perfection—it means returning to understanding again and again. Each time you pause, listen, and stay curious, you strengthen the bond that holds your relationship together.

Tomorrow begins Week 3 — Everyday Connection!

*"Marriage lets you annoy one special
person for the rest of your life."*
**— Anonymous**

# WEEK 3

# EVERYDAY CONNECTION

# Week 3: Everyday Connection

Couples often tell me, "Matt, we just need to learn how to communicate better." And I get it—most of us think communication is the key to a healthy relationship. But the truth is, better communication doesn't always start with words. It starts with connection. A couple who can connect first will naturally communicate better.

*Connect before you correct.*

We're often quick to correct our partner before we've truly connected with them, aren't we? We rush to fix, advise, or demand change before taking the time to slow down and tune in. Connection says, "I see you instead of trying to change you."

Communication is often seen as the foundation of any strong relationship, but real intimacy goes beyond the exchange of information—it's about emotional presence. As John Howard said, "Communication is an exchange of information, but connection is an exchange of humanity." Connection is the heartbeat that makes every conversation feel safe and meaningful.

This week, we'll focus on cultivating that kind of connection—the kind that grows through vulnerability, emotional closeness, and empathy by utilizing language and tools from Dr. John Gottman. True connection means moving past surface-level exchanges to create space where both partners feel seen, valued, and understood. It's not about getting it perfect; it's about consistently showing up with openness and curiosity, even when it feels uncomfortable.

Vulnerability is the bridge that takes us there. It allows us to lower our defenses, share our authentic selves, and invite our partner to do the same. When we choose to be vulnerable, we say, "You matter enough for me to be real."

Throughout this week's exercises, you'll practice connecting before you communicate—learning to listen not just with your ears but with your heart. You'll explore how to respond to each other's emotions with empathy and understanding, how to be emotionally available, and how to transform everyday moments into opportunities for closeness.

Let's move beyond simply talking and step into truly connecting—turning ordinary interactions into sacred moments of understanding that strengthen the bond you've already begun to rebuild.

# Day 15: Identifying Current Connections

When Amber and I were first married, I didn't realize how many simple moments could hold the power of connection. For years, she'd invite me to join her on walks or workouts, and I'd usually say no. It wasn't that I didn't love her—I just didn't see those moments as opportunities to connect. Exercise felt like her thing, not ours.

Over time, though, I began to notice something deeper beneath those invitations. For Amber, movement wasn't just about fitness—it was about *us*. It was time to talk, to laugh, to share something that filled her soul. Every "no" I gave wasn't just about skipping a workout—it was a quiet rejection of togetherness.

Eventually, something shifted in me. I decided to say "yes." At first, it was just a walk here or there, but it grew into something meaningful. Those shared moments became our rhythm—time to breathe, talk, and sometimes say nothing at all. It wasn't about exercise anymore; it was about connection. And somewhere along the way, she told me something that stuck: *"I think it's sexy when you take care of yourself."*

That moment taught me that connection doesn't always look emotional on the surface—it's often found in the small, consistent ways we show up. What might feel ordinary can actually be the heartbeat of your relationship.

## Reflect

How do you currently connect with your partner? Check all that apply:

☐ Emotionally

☐ Spiritually

☐ Socially

- ☐ Intellectually
- ☐ Physically
- ☐ Recreationally
- ☐ Sexually
- ☐ Financially
- ☐ Creatively
- ☐ Parentally

## Engage

Write down one way you could deepen connection in one of these areas this week. Maybe it's cooking a meal together, taking a walk, sharing music, or simply sitting close without distractions.

_____

## Prompt

"I feel most connected to you when we/you _____
_____ because it makes me feel _____
_____."

## Share

After sharing, reflect on what you learned. Did your partner's answer surprise you? How can you create more of these moments intentionally?

**RelationTip:** Connection rarely happens in grand gestures—it grows in the small moments you choose to show up. Consistency builds safety; presence builds trust.

# Day 16: Small Moments, Big Impact

*"It's the small things done often that make the biggest difference in relationships."*
— **Dr. John Gottman**

When most couples think about improving their relationship, they imagine grand gestures — weekend getaways, long talks, or romantic surprises. Those moments matter, but what builds lasting love are the small, daily ways we turn toward each other.

John Gottman calls these *bids for connection* — little gestures, glances, touches, or words that say, *"Will you be here with me?"* Every day, couples make dozens of these bids without even realizing it: a sigh after a long day, a quick text, a playful smile, or a comment about something that happened at work. Each one is an invitation to connect.

When we respond with interest or warmth — by turning toward our partner — we strengthen trust and emotional safety. But when we miss or ignore those bids, even unintentionally, it can leave our partner feeling alone in the relationship. Over time, that creates emotional distance. The good news? Repair begins in awareness. You don't have to respond perfectly — just consistently.

Connection doesn't always come from deep conversation; it often starts with simple presence — a look that says *"I see you,"* a touch that says *"I'm here,"* or a shared laugh that says *"We're still us."*

## Reflect

Think about the small moments that make you feel most connected to your partner. Is it a text during the day? A shared meal? A hug before bed? What do those gestures mean to you?

## Engage

Jot down a moment that made you feel really connected to your partner.

_____

_____

_____

## Prompt

"One small way I can turn toward you more often is by _____ because I know it helps you feel _____."

## Share

Before ending the day, talk briefly about what you plan to notice tomorrow. You might say, "I'm going to look for moments when you reach out so I can be more intentional in how I respond." Or, "I want to practice slowing down and turning toward you, even in small ways." Keep this conversation light, curious, and hopeful — it's about setting an intention together, not measuring success.

**RelationTip:** Love grows in micro-moments. Every time you turn toward your partner — even in the smallest way — you're building trust that lasts a lifetime.

# Day 17: Turning Toward Instead of Away

*"Trust is built in very small moments when our partner is there for us—when they turn toward us in times of need."*
**— Dr. John Gottman**

Every couple faces moments of tension — a misunderstanding, a sharp tone, or a stressful day that spills over into the evening. These moments may seem small, but they matter deeply. When your partner reaches for you in distress, how you respond determines whether the bond between you strengthens or stretches thin.

Turning toward your partner means meeting their bids for connection — especially when it's hard. It's choosing curiosity over defensiveness, empathy over avoidance, and presence over withdrawal. It's not about having the perfect response, but about showing up.

When we turn away, we don't just ignore the moment — we send an unintended message: *"You're alone in this."* That message, repeated over time, can erode trust. But when we turn toward, we say: *"I'm here. You matter. We're in this together."*

Amber and I have learned that the power of repair doesn't come from solving the problem instantly — it comes from staying present through it. There are still moments when one of us feels hurt or misunderstood, but now, instead of shutting down or pushing too hard, we've learned to slow down, breathe, and reach out. Sometimes all it takes is a touch, a look, or a quiet, "I'm with you."

Turning toward isn't always easy, but it's always worth it. Every time you do, you're laying another brick in the foundation of safety and trust that your relationship stands on.

## Reflect

Think about a recent moment of conflict or stress where your partner turned toward you, rather than away. How did it feel?

## Engage

Write down how it felt for your partner to turn toward you in a moment when you needed them:

_____

_____

_____

## Prompt

"One way I can turn toward you more often is by _____ _____ because I know it helps you feel _____ _____."

## Share

Discuss the moment you wrote under "engage". Open up about that moment. What did that look like? How did it make you feel? How can you offer that same presence in return?

**RelationTip:** Turning toward your partner doesn't mean fixing their feelings — it means standing with them in them. Presence is often the most healing response of all.

# Day 18: Rituals of Connection

*"The quality of your rituals determines*
*the quality of your relationship."*
**— Dr. John Gottman**

Connection isn't something we stumble into—it's something we build, one intentional moment at a time. While spontaneity adds fun and freshness, it's the predictable, reliable moments of connection that create a deep sense of safety in a relationship.

Gottman calls these *rituals of connection*—simple, repeated interactions that strengthen your bond. They're the daily, weekly, or seasonal rhythms that say, *"We're still us."* It might be a morning coffee together before the day starts, a goodnight kiss, a Sunday walk, or a shared check-in at the end of each week. These small rituals form the heartbeat of emotional security.

In our home, Amber and I have a few that anchor us. We start each morning at 4am with coffee and catching up, sharing funny memes, or dreaming about our lives. We discuss parenting, laugh together, or discuss what's heavy on our heart. Once the day is over, work is done, and the dinner puzzle has been solved, we watch our favorite sitcom before bed. These are the rituals that we look forward to each day. These rituals have changed or morphed over the years, and I suspect our current rituals will as well. That's expected. But this cannot be left to chance. Rituals are intentional.

Rituals of connection create predictability in a world that constantly changes. They communicate love through consistency. They tell your partner, *"You can count on me."*

## Reflect

Think about your current routines. Are there moments—small or large—that already serve as rituals of connection? What makes those moments meaningful to you?

## Engage

Choose one ritual you'd like to keep or begin together. Write it out here: _____

_____

_____

_____

## Prompt

"One ritual I'd like to keep or create with you is _____

_____ because it will help us stay connected even

when _____."

## Share

Talk about what your ritual will look like. What will help you stay consistent? What might get in the way? How can you gently hold each other accountable to this new rhythm of connection?

**RelationTip:** Love grows in routine. When you create rituals of connection, you're not just adding structure—you're building safety, trust, and belonging. Predictability creates peace.

# Day 19: Shared Joy and Playfulness

*"Couples who laugh together, last together."*
**— Dr. John Gottman**

Joy and playfulness aren't luxuries in love—they're lifelines. In the early days of a relationship, laughter comes easily. But as responsibilities pile up—kids, work, bills, stress—those lighthearted moments often fade into the background. Yet research shows that shared joy strengthens resilience, deepens emotional bonds, and even helps couples recover faster from conflict (Gottman, 1999; Gottman & Gottman, 2017).

Psychologist Barbara Fredrickson (2001, 2009), a leading researcher on positive emotions, found that moments of shared joy expand our capacity for empathy and connection. Her *broaden-and-build theory* explains that positive emotions help us open up, see each other more clearly, and build lasting emotional resources that protect the relationship over time.

From a physiological perspective, play and laughter activate the nervous system's social engagement response—signaling safety, trust, and connection (Porges, 2011). When we share laughter, we're not just having fun; we're literally wiring our brains and bodies for closeness. Simply put: when we laugh together, we heal together.

Amber and I learned this the hard way. In the heavy years—the ones filled with tension, therapy, and rebuilding trust—humor was often the first thing to disappear. But when it returned, even in small doses, it became medicine. A shared laugh after an argument, a silly nickname, or a spontaneous dance in the kitchen reminded us that love doesn't have to be so serious all the time. Play softened the edges. It brought us back to us.

Play is a sacred form of connection—it disarms shame, restores safety, and makes space for joy to return where fear once lived.

## Reflect

When was the last time you and your partner genuinely laughed together? What made that moment so freeing?

## Engage

Plan one simple, playful moment this week and write it down—something that brings joy or lightness to your connection. It could be dancing to your wedding song, playing a board game, cooking together, or revisiting a favorite memory.

_____

_____

_____

## Prompt

"One way I'd like to bring more playfulness into our relationship is by _____ might helps us feel _____."

## Share

Talk about what kind of fun feels most natural to you. What makes you laugh or feel lighthearted together? You might say, "I miss when we used to…" or "It always feels good when we…" The goal isn't to schedule joy—it's to remember what it feels like. Share a few ideas tonight, then choose one small moment this week to bring it to life.

**RelationTip:** Laughter is love's reset button. When you play, you remind your nervous system—and each other—that it's safe to relax, connect, and be fully alive again.

# Day 20: The Power of Presence

*"Being heard is so close to being loved that for the average person, they are almost indistinguishable."*
**— David Augsburger**

We live in a noisy world—texts, notifications, constant demands—all pulling our attention away from the people right in front of us. But the truth is, one of the greatest gifts you can give your partner isn't advice, solutions, or even words. It's your *presence*.

Presence means slowing down enough to notice—the look in your partner's eyes, the tone in their voice, the way they shift when something hurts. It's about showing up fully, body and heart, without trying to fix or control the moment. When you are present, your partner feels it—not just in your words, but in your posture, your breath, your willingness to *stay*.

Amber and I have learned that presence is love made visible. Some of our most healing moments have come not from talking, but from simply *being*—sitting side by side after a hard conversation, holding hands in silence, or taking a quiet walk when words felt too heavy. Those moments reminded us that connection isn't about doing—it's about being with.

When you practice presence, you communicate something powerful: "I see you. I'm not leaving. You matter."

## Reflect

Think about a time when your partner's presence—without words or solutions—made you feel seen or comforted. What made that moment meaningful to you?

## Engage

Today, practice mindful connection. Sit with your partner for five minutes in quiet presence—no phones, no distractions. Simply notice each other. Breathe. Let yourself be seen and see them in return. Write down what that felt like: _____

_____

_____

_____.

## Prompt

"When you're fully present with me, I feel _____

_____ because _____."

## Share

Talk about what that moment of quiet presence felt like. Was it easy? Uncomfortable? Peaceful? Discuss what helps each of you feel *seen* and *known* in daily life.

**RelationTip:** Presence is love in slow motion. The more fully you show up in the ordinary moments, the more extraordinary your connection becomes.

# Day 21: Connection Reflection

Reflection is a powerful tool for growth. As we conclude this week, let's take a moment to intentionally reflect on the connections you made and the insights you gained.

## Reflect

Think back on each day of this week's work. How did you connect with your partner? What stood out to you? Reflect on what it was like to be intentional about strengthening your bond instead of leaving it to chance.

## Engage

Write your thoughts here from your reflection time.

_____

_____

_____

## Prompt

Complete one or more of the following reflections together:

"This week, I noticed that when we _____, our connection felt stronger."

"One thing I learned about you (or myself) this week is _____ _____."

"The part of this week's work I want to carry forward is
_____ because _____."

## Share

Share a simple summary of your reflections with your partner. You don't need to overthink it—just a few words can capture what this week meant to you.

Practice empathetic listening as your partner shares. Try to resist the urge to respond right away. Instead, focus on hearing and understanding their experience.

**RelationTip:** Listening is an act of love. Offering your full attention without interruption creates space for deeper connection.

Week 4, here we come!

*"Marriage is not just spiritual communion; it is also remembering to take out the trash."*
— **Joyce Brothers**

# WEEK 4

# HERE WE GO AGAIN

# Week 4: Here We Go Again

Have you ever thought, *"Here we go again..."*—that sinking feeling just before the conversation even begins? The tension rises, the air shifts, and suddenly you're both back in a familiar loop. Most couples know that moment well. It's the uneasy sense that you've been here before—arguing about the same thing in different forms, circling the same painful dance.

Sue Johnson calls this pattern the *negative cycle*—the looping conversation that turns two people who love each other into opponents instead of allies.

Here's the truth: conflict doesn't ruin relationships. The cycle does. Couples rarely fall apart because they fight too much; they drift apart because they get stuck in a repetitive pattern where neither person feels heard, seen, or safe.

That pattern often takes the shape of the **pursue/withdraw cycle**—one partner moves toward the other, seeking closeness or resolution, while the other steps back, seeking space or safety (Johnson, 2008). Both are trying to protect the relationship in their own way, yet both end up missing each other in the very moments they most need connection.

This week, we're not just identifying the cycle—we're learning how to change it.

Up to this point, you've explored your attachment style, your needs for emotional safety, and the ways you reach for or retreat from connection. All of that groundwork matters, because it helps you see the deeper story beneath your reactions. Now, we'll use that insight to slow down the moments of disconnection and begin to understand what's really happening underneath.

Beneath every argument, silence, or surge of tension lies something far more vulnerable: emotion and need. The pursuer's intensity often hides a fear of being abandoned. The withdrawer's distance often hides a fear of failure or rejection. These aren't flaws—they're protective instincts (Bowlby, 1988; Johnson, 2019). They developed to keep you safe when love once felt uncertain. But when fear leads the dance, love can't find its footing.

Here's the shift: when you begin to see the *cycle* as the problem—not your partner—it changes everything. Blame turns into curiosity. Defensiveness softens into understanding. What once felt like opposition begins to feel like teamwork. Together, you can start to move from disconnection toward repair.

This week, you'll practice noticing the moment your cycle begins to spin. You'll learn to name your positions, identify your triggers, and pause long enough to speak from the softer, truer emotions underneath—fear, sadness, longing, love. Because when we speak from the heart instead of our defenses, we create safety where tension once lived.

Every couple has a cycle. The difference between those who grow together and those who fall apart is whether they learn to name and repair.

When you can interrupt your cycle with care instead of control—with tenderness instead of tension—you begin to form a new pattern: one grounded in safety, trust, and connection.

You've done the work of understanding yourself and your needs. Now, it's time to bring that awareness into the moments that matter most. Let's slow the dance. Let's name it, understand it, and begin the brave work of breaking it—side by side.

# Day 22: Our Dance

*"Conflict is inevitable in any relationship, but how we handle it determines whether it drives us apart or brings us closer together."*
**— Dr. John Gottman**

Every couple experiences tension—it's part of being two different people trying to build one shared life. What matters most is how we navigate those moments of disconnection. In emotionally charged situations, most couples fall into what's known as the **pursue/withdraw dynamic**—a dance where one partner reaches for closeness while the other steps back to find safety (Johnson, 2008).

The pursuer often feels anxious when emotional distance grows. They crave conversation, reassurance, and resolution. Their pursuit isn't about control—it's about longing. They want to know the relationship is still okay. The withdrawer, on the other hand, often feels overwhelmed by intensity or pressure. Pulling back becomes a way to protect both themselves and the relationship from further conflict or emotional flooding (Johnson, 2019). Their silence isn't rejection—it's regulation.

Both roles are rooted in care and protection, but when left unchecked, this pattern creates a painful cycle: the more one pursues, the more the other withdraws, leaving both partners unseen and misunderstood. Over time, what began as an effort to connect can start to feel like the very thing that drives you apart.

The goal of this exercise isn't to eliminate conflict or label one partner as "right" or "wrong." It's to recognize the cycle—to name it before it takes over. When you can pause, reflect, and speak from softer emotions—fear, sadness, longing, or love—you move from defensiveness to connection. That's where healing begins (Johnson, 2008).

## Reflect

When conflict arises, what are the internal messages you begin to hear or feel? Do you tend to pursue for clarity and connection, or withdraw to protect and avoid escalation?

## Engage

Spend time writing down how you normally hand conflict. Do you identify more with the pursuer or the withdrawer?

_____

_____

_____

## Prompt

"I think I tend to show up in our relationship as more of the _____ (pursuer or withdrawer)."

## Share

Take turns sharing your answer from above and what you notice about how it impacts your cycle as a couple. Talk about one small way you could each show up differently moving forward.
This isn't a time for blame or criticism—it's an opportunity for awareness and personal ownership. As you listen, thank your partner for being honest, and remind each other that understanding the pattern is the first step toward changing it.

**RelationTip:** You don't need to trade roles—you need to understand them. Pursuers seek safety through connection. Withdrawers seek safety through space. Both are valid. Compassion lives in the space between.

# Day 23: Owning Your Role in the Cycle

*"It's not you against your partner—*
*it's both of you against the cycle."*
— **Sue Johnson**

Every couple has a pattern that shows up when disconnection happens. One partner tends to move toward, seeking reassurance or clarity, while the other pulls back to find calm or protection. These responses are instinctive—they're not flaws or failures, but strategies rooted in attachment and self-preservation (Bowlby, 1988; Johnson, 2008).

Owning your role in the cycle doesn't mean taking all the blame. It means recognizing how your actions—both big and small—can feed the loop. The moment you can pause and say, "I see my part in this," you shift from reactivity to responsibility. That's the beginning of change (Johnson, 2019).

When both partners take ownership, something powerful happens: **the cycle loses control**. You stop fighting to be right and start fighting to reconnect.

## Reflect

Think about a recent disagreement. What did you tend to do when things got tense—move toward your partner or away from them?

## Engage

Write your typical role in the cycle. Use language like:

"When I feel _____, I tend to _____, and that often makes you _____."

## Prompt

"One way I can take ownership of my role in our cycle is by _____ because I want to create more safety and connection between us."

## Share

Take turns acknowledging what you each bring to the pattern. Offer appreciation for your partner's honesty, even if it's hard to hear. This isn't about guilt—it's about growth.

**RelationTip:** Awareness is the first step to transformation. When you own your part of the pattern, you reclaim the power to change it—and invite your partner to do the same.

# Day 24: Name It to Tame It

*"When you can name your negative cycle together, you take away its power to define your connection."*
— **Sue Johnson**

Once you've learned to recognize your role in conflict, the next step is to name the cycle itself. This is the dance that happens when both partners' instincts collide—one reaches, the other retreats, and both feel unseen or unsafe (Johnson, 2008).

Naming your cycle is one of the most powerful things you can do for your relationship. It turns the pattern into something external—a shared challenge instead of a personal flaw. When you name it, you make it visible. You give yourselves a way to say, "I think our cycle is showing up," instead of "You're doing that thing again."

Some couples even give their cycle a nickname—something that helps them recognize it without shame or blame. Whether you call it *The Chase*, *The Storm*, *The Shutdown*, or something entirely your own, the goal is to see it for what it is: an automatic loop that no longer gets to run your relationship (Johnson, 2019).

## Reflect

Think about your last few conflicts. What usually happens first? Who tends to move toward? Who tends to pull away? What emotions are underneath those reactions—fear, sadness, frustration, shame, longing?

## Engage

Write out your pattern using simple language: "When you
_____, I _____, and then you _____, and around
and around we go."

Be gentle and curious as you fill this in together. There's no right or
wrong answer—just shared awareness.

## Prompt

"What if we gave our cycle a name? Something that helps us recognize it and interrupt it sooner. We could call it _____
_____."

## Share

Talk about what it feels like to have a name for your pattern/cycle.
Do you find relief in knowing it's about you or your partner, but
about the cycle?

**RelationTip:** When you name your cycle, you're no longer enemies—you're teammates. The goal isn't to win against each other,
but to win against the pattern that keeps you disconnected.

# Day 25: Raw Spots

Now that you have named your cycle, let's go further into what sets the cycle in motion: Raw Spots.

> *"Our raw spots are like emotional bruises—*
> *when they get bumped, we react more to*
> *the pain inside than the moment itself."*
> **— Sue Johnson**

Every person carries emotional raw spots—tender places shaped by past experiences, unmet needs, or moments of disconnection. These raw spots can turn small misunderstandings into big reactions (*the cycle*) because they touch something deeper—something old (Johnson, 2008).

Maybe your raw spot is feeling unheard, unseen, or unimportant. Maybe it's the fear of being left or the belief that your needs don't matter. Whatever it is, these triggers are not weaknesses—they're signals. They point to where healing is needed most (Johnson, 2019).

When you and your partner can identify these raw spots, you gain insight into what's really happening beneath the surface and can slow and even stop your negative cycle before it takes over. Instead of reacting to the words being said, you begin to respond to the feelings underneath. That's how emotional safety grows—through awareness, empathy, and gentleness.

## Reflect

Think about a recent moment when your negative cycle took over. What raw spot got "bumped" inside you? What did that moment remind you of from earlier in your life or relationship?

## Engage

Write out what happened inside you when that raw spot got bumped:

_____

_____

_____

## Prompt

"One raw spot I've noticed in myself is _____

because it touches an old feeling of _____."

## Share

Take turns reflecting on how these raw spots might influence your cycle. What compassion could you offer your partner the next time you see their raw spot being touched?

**RelationTip:** When you can see your partner's raw spot, you begin to see their pain—not their defenses.

# Day 26: Caring for Raw Spots

Naming a raw spot is only the beginning. The next step is learning how to care for it—with gentleness, patience, and curiosity. When you or your partner get emotionally "bumped," the goal isn't to avoid the pain; it's to bring comfort and care to the place that hurts.

Sue Johnson calls this the essence of repair—when one partner reaches toward the other with empathy, it helps transform pain into closeness. Raw spots don't disappear overnight, but when they're met with understanding instead of judgment, they begin to soften.

Caring for each other's raw spots means remembering that every reaction has a story behind it. The anger, silence, or tears aren't the whole truth—they're protective responses to pain that once felt too big to bear alone. Healing happens when those moments are met with safety rather than shame.

When your partner's raw spot gets touched:

- **Pause before reacting.** Take a breath and notice what's happening inside both of you.
- **Name what you see.** "This feels like a tender spot for you. I want to understand."
- **Offer comfort instead of correction.** A gentle tone, a soft gaze, or a hand on the shoulder says more than a thousand explanations.

Emotional safety deepens when partners learn to *become the balm* instead of the bruise.

## Reflect

Think about a time when your partner's raw spot was touched and you saw their pain surface. How did you respond? What could you do differently next time to help them feel safe instead of alone?

## Engage

Write down one thing that helps you feel soothed when your own raw spot is activated—and one thing that seems to soothe your partner.

1.  Something that comforts *me*: _____

    _____.

2.  Something that comforts *my partner*: _____

    _____.

## Prompt

"When I notice your raw spot being touched, I want to remember to

_____ because I know that underneath,

you're really feeling _____."

## Share

Take turns reading your prompt aloud. As your partner shares, simply listen. Then, reflect back what you heard using soft language like,

*   "That makes sense—you just want to feel seen when that happens."
*   "I didn't realize how deep that goes for you. Thank you for trusting me with it."

Afterward, talk about one small action you can each take when raw spots show up again—something that communicates, *"I'm here, and we're okay."*

**RelationTip:** Raw spots don't need fixing—they need *holding*. When you respond to each other's tenderness with care instead of criticism, you're rewriting the story of safety together.

# Day 27: Speaking from Softer Emotions

*"When we share the softer feelings beneath our anger or defensiveness, we invite our partner into our inner world— and that's where connection begins."*
— **Sue Johnson**

Most conflict doesn't start with anger—it starts with hurt. But anger is easier to express than fear, sadness, or loneliness. Those deeper emotions often stay hidden because they make us feel exposed. Yet those are the very feelings that foster closeness when shared gently (Johnson, 2008).

In Emotionally Focused Therapy, this shift is called moving from *secondary emotions*—the ones that protect us, like frustration or defensiveness—to *primary emotions*—the ones that connect us, like fear, sadness, or longing (Johnson, 2019). The surface emotion says, "I'm protecting myself." The deeper one says, "I need you." When you speak from that softer place, you give your partner a glimpse of what's really happening inside—and that opens the door to empathy instead of escalation.

Expressing vulnerability isn't weakness. It's courage. It's saying, "I trust you enough to show you my heart." And when you do, you make space for your partner to do the same.

## Reflect

Go back to your familiar pattern from day 24. When that pattern engages, what emotion shows up first—anger, frustration, silence, sarcasm? Now look underneath it. What softer feeling was hiding there—hurt, fear, loneliness, shame, longing?

## Engage

Before sharing, write out what tends to happen for you in those moments. You can use language like: "When I feel _____

_____, I often react by _____. But underneath, what I really feel is _____."

Example: "When I feel rejected, I often react by getting defensive or shutting down. But underneath, what I really feel is hurt and afraid that I don't matter to you."

## Prompt

"If I'm honest, when we go round and round, the softer part of me wants you to know that I feel _____.

If I could share this with you in the moment, I know we would feel closer."

Here's a list of softer emotions to help you: Fear, sadness, loneliness, shame, hurt, longing, insecurity, helplessness, vulnerability, yearning.

## Share

Talk together about what it was like to express a softer emotion instead of one with an edge. How did it feel to let your guard down and speak from that gentler place? Notice what shifted between you when you did.

**RelationTip:** Vulnerability is not weakness—it's wisdom. When you speak from your heart instead of your defenses, you stop fighting to be right and start fighting for connection.

# Day 28: Seeing the Pattern Clearly

When you can step back and see your cycle for what it is, something powerful happens—the problem stops being *you versus your partner* and becomes *both of you versus the pattern.*

Over the past few days, you've named your triggers, raw spots, and protective moves. Today is about pulling those threads together—seeing how they connect and influence each other. When a raw spot gets touched, it activates emotion; emotion drives reaction; reaction pulls the other into their own pattern. And before you know it, you're both caught in a loop you never wanted to be in.

The good news? You can interrupt that loop. Every time you recognize what's happening and name it with kindness—"There's our cycle again" or "That hit a tender spot for me"—you reclaim control from the pattern and put it back in your hands as a couple. As Sue Johnson reminds us, naming the dance is the first step toward changing it (Johnson, 2008).

## Reflect

Think of the last time your cycle took over. What was the sequence? What got triggered first—your emotion, your partner's move, or your own raw spot? How did it escalate?

## Engage

Write out and underline or circle the parts of the cycle that link directly to your raw spots. Ask yourself: What fear or story was underneath that moment? What did I need but didn't know how to ask for? How did my reaction affect my partner's raw spot in return?

_____

_____

_____

## Prompt

"When our cycle starts, my raw spot usually gets touched when _____. That's when I tend to _____, which often makes you feel _____. What I'm learning is that underneath it all, I really need _____."

Example: "When our cycle starts, my raw spot usually gets touched when you pull away during conflict. That's when I tend to get louder and push harder for connection, which often makes you feel cornered and shut down. What I'm learning is that underneath it all, I really need reassurance that we're okay—that even when we disagree, you still want to work through it with me."

## Share

Take turns reading your reflections. When your partner shares, practice empathy and curiosity—try to see the moment from *their* raw spot. You might say, "I can see how that story gets activated for you." or "That makes sense, given what you've been through." or "I didn't realize that my reaction touched something so deep. Thank you for helping me see it." As you share, remember: this is not about blame—it's about understanding the emotional logic behind your patterns.

**RelationTip:** When you can both see the cycle and the raw spots that fuel it, you no longer feel like enemies. You become allies against the pattern. Awareness turns conflict into collaboration, and collaboration builds safety.

# WEEK 5

# TAMING THE FOUR HORSEMEN

# Week 5: Taming the Four Horsemen

By now, you've seen how disconnection often begins—not with malice, but with misunderstanding. When emotions run high, even loving partners can slip into patterns that protect rather than connect. Over time, these patterns start to shape the way we talk, listen, and respond to one another.

Drs. John and Julie Gottman discovered that certain communication habits are especially corrosive to connection. They called them *The Four Horsemen of the Apocalypse*—criticism, defensiveness, contempt, and stonewalling—because when these behaviors take over, they predict relational breakdown with striking accuracy (Gottman & Silver, 2015).

Each Horseman represents a specific way we protect ourselves when we feel hurt, unheard, or misunderstood:

- **Criticism** – Attacking your partner's character instead of naming a behavior.
  *"You always…"* or *"You never…"* This sets a negative tone and is often the first sign of trouble.

- **Contempt** – Mocking, eye-rolling, sarcasm, or name-calling. Contempt is the most dangerous Horseman and the single greatest predictor of divorce. It communicates disgust and superiority.

- **Defensiveness** – Protecting yourself by playing the victim, counterattacking, or deflecting responsibility. While it may start as self-protection, it quickly escalates conflict instead of calming it.

- **Stonewalling** – Withdrawing, shutting down, or going silent. This usually happens when one partner feels physiologically overwhelmed or *"flooded."* It creates emotional distance and stalls repair (Gottman, 1999).

But here's the hopeful truth: each of these behaviors has an **antidote**—a way to return to connection and safety:

- Criticism → Gentle Start-Up
- Contempt → Building a Culture of Appreciation
- Defensiveness → Taking Responsibility
- Stonewalling → Self-Soothing

We'll continue to use the **REPS** model (*Reflect, Engage, Prompt, Share*) to explore these patterns one by one. You'll learn to recognize them in real time, understand where they originate in your story, and practice healthy responses that strengthen trust instead of tearing it down.

Conflict doesn't have to be a threat to your relationship—it can be a doorway to deeper intimacy, compassion, and repair.

# Day 29: Criticism

This week, we're exploring The Four Horsemen identified by Drs. John and Julie Gottman—Criticism, Contempt, Defensiveness, and Stonewalling (Gottman, 1999). Each of these patterns can quietly erode trust, intimacy, and safety in a relationship if left unchecked.

Today, we begin with **Criticism**—one of the most common and subtle Horsemen to show up. Criticism happens when we attack our partner's character instead of addressing a specific behavior or expressing a clear need. It often begins with words like *"You always"* or *"You never"* and carries an underlying tone of blame.

It might sound like:

- "You always interrupt me when I'm talking."
- "You never think about anyone but yourself."
- "You only care about what you want."

Criticism doesn't invite understanding—it builds defensiveness and distance. It says, *"You're the problem,"* instead of *"There's a problem between us."*

The antidote to criticism is a **gentle start-up**—beginning conversations with *"I" statements* that express how you feel and what you need without blame (Gottman & Silver, 2015). When you speak from your own emotions instead of pointing the finger, you keep the door open for empathy, not escalation.

Let's walk through today's exercise using the REPS model.

## Reflect

Think back to a time when you criticized your partner. What was happening in the moment? What need were you trying to express— but perhaps it came out as blame?

## Engage

Invite your partner into a calm conversation about how criticism shows up in your relationship. Ask them what it feels like when criticism is directed at them—and listen. Your goal isn't to defend your actions, but to understand their emotional experience.

Try asking:

- "When I criticize or sound harsh, what does that bring up for you?"
- "Can you tell me how you feel in those moments?"

## Prompt

Let's practice shifting from criticism to clarity. Below are a few examples of criticism turned into "I" statements:

- **Criticism:** "You never help around the house."
  → "I feel overwhelmed when the chores fall on me. I need us to find a better balance."
- **Criticism:** "You always interrupt me!"
  → "I feel unheard when I'm interrupted. It would mean a lot to me if you let me finish before jumping in."

Now try creating a few of your own:

I would normally say: "You _____ "

Turn that into an "I" statement:

"I feel _____ _____ when

_____ because _____."

## Share

Take a few minutes to share your commitment to reducing criticism in your relationship. Talk with your partner about one way you plan to express yourself with more care, honesty, and kindness.

You might say: *"I know criticism has crept into the way I speak sometimes. I want to do better. I'm committed to speaking from my heart, not from frustration."*

**RelationTip:** Criticism is easy; love is hard. But the more we speak with intention, the more our relationship becomes a place where both people feel heard and respected.

# Day 30: Contempt

If **criticism** is the spark that starts disconnection, **contempt** is the wildfire that burns trust.

Contempt shows up when we feel superior—rolling our eyes, using sarcasm, or mocking our partner's faults. It often hides deeper pain: the exhaustion of feeling unseen or unheard for too long. When contempt enters the room, empathy leaves.

Dr. John Gottman calls *contempt the single greatest predictor of divorce* (Gottman, 1999) because it conveys disgust instead of respect. But there's an antidote—**building a culture of appreciation.** Appreciation softens contempt by shifting our focus from what's missing to what's good. It reminds us that love grows when gratitude is spoken out loud.

When we choose to appreciate instead of criticize, we say to our partner, *"You matter to me, even when we disagree."*

## Reflect

Think of a recent moment when you felt contempt rise up—a sigh, an eye-roll, a sarcastic comment. What was happening underneath? Were you hurt, disappointed, or lonely?
What would you have needed in that moment to stay open instead of pulling away?

## Engage

Talk with your partner about how contempt shows up in your relationship.
Ask gently:

- "What does it feel like when I'm sarcastic or critical?"

- "Are there moments when you feel disrespected or dismissed?"

Listen to understand, not to justify. Then switch roles.

## Prompt

Now let's replace contempt with appreciation.

Write down three specific things you value about your partner—qualities, efforts, or moments that made you feel grateful.

1. I appreciate you for _____

2. I felt cared for when _____

3. One thing I admire about you is _____

When you're done, read them out loud to each other.

_____

_____

_____

## Examples of the shift:

- **Contempt:** "You're impossible to talk to."
  → **Appreciation:** "I really value how you try to stay calm when we disagree."

- **Contempt:** "Must be nice to relax while I do everything."
  → **Appreciation:** "I notice how hard you've been working lately—I could use some teamwork tonight."

- **Contempt:** "You're so dramatic."
  → **Appreciation:** "I know emotions run high sometimes. I'm glad you care enough to feel deeply."

## Share

Exchange your lists and talk about what it was like to hear appreciation spoken directly.
Did anything surprise you? How did your body respond—did you feel yourself soften?

Commit to naming one thing you appreciate about your partner every day this week, even something small.

**RelationTip:** Contempt erodes connection, but appreciation rebuilds it brick by brick. When you intentionally look for what's good and speak it out loud, you re-teach your nervous system that your partner is an ally, not an adversary. Gratitude isn't denial of what's hard—it's choosing to keep love in the room while you work through it.

# Day 31: Defensiveness

When we feel misunderstood or accused, defensiveness can rise fast. It's our nervous system's way of saying, "I don't feel safe." We protect ourselves by explaining, justifying, or turning the tables—but in doing so, we miss the chance to connect.

Defensiveness often sounds like:

- "That's not what I said!"
- "You do the same thing!"
- "I was only trying to help."

The intention is protection, but the impact is disconnection.

So what is the antidote to defensiveness? **Taking responsibility.**

Taking responsibility doesn't mean accepting all the blame—it means acknowledging your part in what happened. It's saying, "I can see how my words or actions affected you, and I want to do better" Responsibility lowers defenses, restores safety, and opens the door to repair (Gottman & Silver, 2012).

## Reflect

Think of a recent argument where you felt defensive.

- What were you trying to protect?
- What emotion was underneath your defense—fear, shame, guilt, or hurt?
- Looking back, is there a small piece you can take responsibility for?

## Engage

Invite your partner into a calm, curious conversation about defensiveness.

Ask:

• "When I get defensive, how does that feel for you?"

• "Is there something I could do differently to make those moments safer?"

Then switch roles. This is not about calling each other out—it's about understanding what happens between you when defenses go up.

## Prompt

Practice shifting from defensiveness to ownership.

Below are examples of common defensive reactions turned into responsibility-taking statements:

• Defensive: "That's not what I meant!"

  → Responsible: "You're right, I could have said that differently. I see how it landed wrong."

• Defensive: "You're just overreacting."

  → Responsible: "I can tell that really affected you. I didn't realize how strong that impact was."

• Defensive: "You're making a big deal out of nothing."

  → Responsible: "I didn't notice how important that was to you. I want to understand it better."

## Now write your own:

"When I would normally say: _____,

I can instead say: _____."

## Share

Take turns sharing what it's like to hear your partner take ownership without excuses or defensiveness. How did it feel? What shifted in your body or heart when they said, "You're right" or "I see how that impacted you"?

Then talk about one small way you each plan to practice responsibility moving forward—even when it feels uncomfortable.

**RelationTip:** Defensiveness protects the ego but hurts the relationship. Responsibility protects the bond (Gottman & Silver, 2015). When you own even a small part of the problem, you create space for your partner to soften too. Repair begins where defense ends.

# Day 32: Stonewalling

When tension rises, some people shut down. The words stop, the eyes drop, the body goes still. Inside, though, everything is racing. This is stonewalling—a protective reaction that happens when your nervous system becomes overwhelmed, flooded with emotion, and no longer able to stay engaged (Gottman, 1999).

Stonewalling isn't always intentional; it's the body's way of saying, "I can't handle any more." But when one partner withdraws and the other keeps pursuing, both end up feeling abandoned and unheard.

The antidote to stonewalling is self-soothing (Gottman & Silver, 2012). Self-soothing means pausing long enough to regulate your body so that you can return to the conversation calm, grounded, and open. It's not running away—it's stepping away to come back better.

## Reflect

Think of a time when you or your partner shut down during conflict.

- What sensations did you notice—tight chest, shallow breath, blank mind?
- What thoughts or fears were underneath?
- How long did it take before you were able to re-engage?

## Engage

Talk with your partner about what it feels like when one of you withdraws.

Ask:

- "What happens for you when I go quiet?"
- "What would help you feel safe if I need to step away?"

Then switch roles. Your goal is to understand each other's internal experience—not to assign blame.

## Prompt

Practice the antidote: Self-Soothing.
When you notice yourself shutting down, try these steps (Gottman & Silver, 2015):

1.  **Pause the conversation kindly.**
    Say, "I'm feeling overwhelmed and need a short break. I promise I'll come back."

2.  **Breathe and move.**
    Take ten slow breaths, stretch, or step outside for fresh air.

3.  **Name what's happening inside.**
    "My chest feels tight; I'm anxious." Naming calms the brain.

4.  **Return and reconnect.**
    After at least 20 minutes, come back and begin with, "Thank you for giving me space. I'm ready to keep talking."

Now, complete this reflection:

"When I notice myself shutting down, it usually means I'm feeling
_____. To help myself stay present, I can
_____. When I'm ready to re-engage, it
helps me when you _____."

## Share

Take turns discussing what self-soothing practices you'll use in future conflicts and how your partner can support you. You might say, "If I tell you I need a break, please trust that I'll come back. It's not avoidance—it's care."

**RelationTip:** Stonewalling says, "I can't stay." Self-soothing says, "I care enough to come back." Learning to regulate yourself in moments of overwhelm keeps the argument from becoming an abandonment (Gottman, 1999). When both partners respect the pause, the relationship becomes a safer place to land.

# Day 33: Turning Conflict into Connection

By now, you've met all four of the Horsemen—**Criticism, Contempt, Defensiveness, and Stonewalling**—and learned their antidotes (Gottman & Silver, 1999). Each skill you practiced was like learning a new instrument. Today, you'll start playing them together—creating harmony where there once was noise.

Repair, curiosity, and empathy rebuild that connection every time you reach for an antidote instead of a reaction.

When you combine the Four Antidotes, your conflicts begin to sound different (Gottman & Silver, 2015):

- You start with a **Gentle Start-Up** instead of Criticism.
- You speak **Appreciation** instead of Contempt.
- You take **Responsibility** instead of getting Defensive.
- You practice **Self-Soothing** instead of Stonewalling.

This is how couples move from survival to safety, from tension to tenderness.

## Reflect

Think about a recent disagreement that didn't go well.
Which Horsemen showed up? Which antidotes could have changed the direction of that conversation?

## Engage

Choose one mild conflict or ongoing tension to revisit together. Before you talk, review the four antidotes.

Take turns practicing:

- **Gentle Start-Up:** "I feel _____ about _____ and I need ____."

- **Appreciation:** "I really value ____ about how you handle ____."
- **Responsibility:** "You're right, I can see my part in that."
- **Self-Soothing:** "I'm getting flooded and need a short break, but I'll come back."

## Prompt

Use the sentence stems below to rehearse a full repair cycle:

1. "When _____ happened, I felt _____ because _____." (*Gentle Start-Up*)
2. "I appreciate that you _____." (*Appreciation*)
3. "I can take responsibility for _____." (*Responsibility*)
4. "Next time I start to shut down, I'll _____ to self-soothe and re-engage." (*Self-Soothing*)

## Share

Take a moment to reflect together:

- What changed when you used these antidotes?
- Did the conversation feel safer or softer?
- Which antidote felt most natural—and which one needs more practice?

End by thanking each other for trying something new. Growth happens in these tiny, intentional turns toward each other.

**RelationTip:** Repair doesn't require perfection—just pattern-breaking (Gottman & Silver, 1999). Each time you use even one antidote, you interrupt the cycle of disconnection. Over time, these small moments of repair become the foundation of lasting trust and intimacy.

# Day 34: The Art of Repair

Even the healthiest couples mess up. Maybe it's saying the wrong thing, misreading a tone, shutting down, or reacting too quickly. The strength of your relationship isn't measured by how few ruptures you have—but by how quickly you repair them.

Repair is the moment you choose to turn back toward your partner instead of away. It's the emotional bridge that transforms conflict into closeness. Dr. John Gottman found that successful couples repair early and often—sometimes mid-conflict—with a simple look, word, or touch that says, "I still care about us" (Gottman & Silver, 1999; 2012).

Repair is not about solving the problem; it's about restoring safety. Once the heart feels safe, the mind can follow (Gottman & Silver, 2015).

## Reflect

Think of a recent moment of tension.

- How long did it take before one of you reached out to reconnect?
- What made it easier—or harder—to move toward repair?
- What signals (body language, tone, timing) told you that safety was returning?

## Engage

Together, look back at that moment and discuss how repair could have happened sooner.

Ask each other:

- "What helps you know I'm ready to reconnect?"

- "What do I do (or say) that helps—or hinders—repair?"
- "How can we let each other know we're ready to come back together?"

## Prompt

Practice a short repair conversation using this prompt:

"I could have reached for repair sooner by _____
_____.

## Share

After your repair, talk about how it felt to reconnect:
- Did the tension ease?
- What helped the most—words, tone, or physical closeness?
- How might you use these steps next time a rupture happens?

**RelationTip:** Repair doesn't erase what happened—it reestablishes *us*. Every time you repair, you remind your partner that the relationship is stronger than the conflict *(Gottman & Silver, 2015)*. The goal isn't to avoid storms; it's to learn how to find each other in the rain.

# Day 35: Integrating Repair and Appreciation

You've spent this week exploring the Four Horsemen and learning their antidotes—Gentle Start-Up, Appreciation, Responsibility, and Self-Soothing (Gottman & Silver, 1999). Each one gives you a new way to protect your bond instead of your pride. Together, they create a culture where safety, softness, and repair come first.

Today is about weaving those practices together—turning what you've learned into daily habits of connection.

## Reflect

Look back over the past week.

- Which antidote felt most natural to you?
- Which one challenged you the most?
- When did you feel most connected while practicing these skills?

## Engage

With your partner, review each antidote briefly and name one example of when you used it.

- Gentle Start-Up – "I approached the conversation calmly instead of accusing."
- Appreciation – "I noticed something good and said it out loud."
- Responsibility – "I owned my part instead of defending."
- Self-Soothing – "I took a break and came back grounded."

Talk about how each of these small moments changed the energy between you.

## Prompt

Create your own "Repair & Appreciation Ritual."
This can be simple—something you practice at the end of a tough day, a disagreement, or a long week.

Use the space below to write a short ritual statement or commitment:

"When tension rises, we will _____."

"Before bed, we will _____."

"Each week, we will name _____ that we appreciate about each other."

## Share

Take turns reading your ritual aloud. Notice how it feels to commit to connection, not perfection. You might seal it with a hug, a hand squeeze, or a simple "thank you for trying."

**RelationTip:** Gratitude and repair are two sides of the same coin—both say, *"I see you, and you matter to me."* When appreciation becomes a daily rhythm, the Four Horsemen lose their power *(Gottman & Silver, 2015)*. Conflict no longer threatens your bond; it strengthens it.

# WEEK 6

# WHAT I REALLY NEED

# Week 6: What I Really Need

*"You are only as needy as your unmet needs."*
— **John Bowlby (as cited in Holmes, 2014)**

Kenny started our session the way he always did—checking in, asking how we were doing. But this time, the air in the room was different. There was a quiet tension neither of us could name. Amber sat back in her chair, arms crossed, eyes distant. I felt a familiar unease in my chest—the sense that something was off, but I didn't know what.

Eventually, it came out. The night before, Amber had been bathing the kids while I sat at the kitchen table, scrolling or working—I can't remember which. It was a scene we'd repeated hundreds of times, and I didn't think twice about it. But for her, something shifted that night. She felt alone, unseen, and tired of carrying the load by herself.

When Kenny gently asked what was happening underneath her frustration, Amber hesitated. Then he said something that stopped both of us in our tracks: "Amber, did you know that you're allowed to ask Matt for help?"

Amber's eyes filled with tears. "No," she said quietly. "I don't ask for help. I just do it alone."

Kenny leaned in. "Where did you learn that?"

That question opened a door neither of us had walked through before. Amber began to realize she'd been taught—long before me—that asking for help meant weakness, that needing something made you a burden. And I began to see how my lack of awareness and her silence created a perfect storm for disconnection.

That moment in therapy changed everything. It wasn't dramatic, but it was defining. We started to see unmet and unspoken needs are the ones that create the distance.

Every person has needs—emotional, physical, spiritual, and relational. Yet many of us have learned to suppress or downplay them, believing they make us weak, needy, or too much. This week, we'll begin rewriting that story.

Understanding and expressing your needs—and learning how to respond to your partner's—are essential steps toward a thriving relationship. We'll continue using the REPS model (Reflect, Engage, Prompt, Share) to help you both locate, communicate, and meet each other's needs without shame or fear.

Amber and I have been married for over two decades, and that moment with Kenny remains one of the most transformative lessons we've ever learned. Amber learned that asking for help didn't make her weak—it made her human. I learned that awareness isn't passive; it's love in motion. Together, we began to practice a new kind of safety: one where needs could be spoken, heard, and met without shame.

That's the heart of this week. Your needs—and your partner's—are not flaws to manage; they're invitations to connection. When we stop hiding our needs and start honoring them, we don't become needy—we become whole.

# Day 36: Identifying Your Own Needs

As I shared in this week's introduction, John Bowlby once said, "You are only as needy as your unmet needs" (as cited in Holmes, 2014). That truth carries weight. When our emotional needs go unacknowledged—by ourselves or by our partner—it quietly breeds frustration, miscommunication, and distance. We start to feel unsettled, unseen, or even "too much."

Ironically, it's not the need itself that makes us feel needy—it's the disconnection around it. When our longings go unnoticed or unspoken, they start to leak out sideways through irritation, withdrawal, or over functioning. Today's work is about bringing those needs into the light—not to judge them, but to understand them.

Today's work is also about slowing down long enough to listen inward.
What do you need most in order to feel safe, loved, and connected?
What do you long for, but often silence?

Below is a list of common emotional needs to help you find language for what may live beneath your reactions or patterns. Highlight or circle 3–5 that deeply resonate with you.

Acceptance | Trust | Honesty | Appreciation | Connection | Forgiveness | Affection | Comfort | Loyalty | Validation | Communication | Peace | Understanding | Autonomy | Vulnerability | Empathy | Playfulness | Recognition | Respect | Support | Stability | Reassurance | Security | Compassion | Encouragement | Intimacy | Openness | Companionship | Belonging | Growth | Safety

## Reflect

Think about a time when your partner met one or more of your emotional needs.

- What happened in that moment?
- How did it affect your emotions, your behavior, and your connection with your partner?

## Engage

Spend some time writing down your top three emotional needs from the list above—or add your own.

1. _____

2. _____

3. _____

## Prompt

Complete this sentence:

"One of my most important needs is

_____ because when it's met, I feel

_____."

## Share

Take turns sharing your top three needs that feel most important right now.
Invite curiosity, not commentary. Allow your partner to ask gentle questions and reflect back what they hear so both of you can feel more understood and attuned.

**RelationTip:** Naming your needs isn't selfish—it's sacred. When you clearly express what helps you feel safe and seen, you're not asking too much; you're offering your partner a map to love you well.

# Day 37: Listening to Your Partner's Needs

When we truly listen to our partner's needs—not just with our ears, but with our presence—we communicate one of the most powerful messages in a relationship: *"You matter. I want to understand you."*

Needs are often layered beneath emotions, behaviors, or even silence. Listening well means slowing down, staying curious, and tuning in without jumping to fix or defend. According to Dr. Sue Johnson, this kind of attuned responsiveness creates emotional safety—the foundation of a secure bond (Johnson, 2008).

Today is about practicing the kind of listening that builds connection, trust, and emotional safety—listening to understand, not to respond.

## Reflect

How do you typically respond when your partner shares a need?
Do you interrupt, defend, minimize, or feel anxious about getting it right?
What would it look like to simply hold space and hear them fully?

## Engage

Invite your partner to share one need that matters deeply to them right now—whether emotional, physical, or relational.

Your only job is to stay grounded, stay open, and reflect back what you hear.

## Prompt

Complete this statement after your partner shares: "What I hear you

saying is that you need_____ because

it helps you feel _____."

Then respond with: "Something I can do to support that need this week is _____."

## Share

Once you've both shared, ask:
"What's one way I can keep showing up for this need going forward?"
Take a moment to thank your partner for being honest and vulnerable.

**RelationTip:** Listening is love in action. When your partner shares a need and you slow down enough to truly hear it, you're not just meeting the need—you're strengthening the bond that holds you together.

# Day 38: Responding to Needs Without Losing Yourself

Healthy love requires balance—being emotionally responsive to your partner while staying rooted in yourself. When one partner continually overextends to meet the other's needs, quiet resentment or exhaustion can begin to grow. On the other hand, when we dismiss or minimize our partner's needs, safety and trust start to erode.

Responding to needs without losing yourself means holding two truths at once:
"Your needs matter."
"And so do mine."

This is the heart of interdependence—where love isn't about sacrifice or self-protection, but mutual respect and emotional balance. As Prentis Hemphill reminds us, boundaries are "the distance at which I can love you and me simultaneously" (Hemphill, 2018). Boundaries aren't a withdrawal of love; they're what allow love to last.

## Reflect

Think of a time when you felt torn between meeting your partner's needs and honoring your own. What made that situation difficult?

## Engage

Identify one recurring need your partner expresses that sometimes feels hard for you to meet. Then, name what *you* need in order to show up for them in a healthy, sustainable way.

Example: "My partner needs reassurance when we argue. I need a moment to calm down first so I can be present."

Write your own version:

"My partner needs _____. I need

_____ so I can meet that need with care."

## Prompt

Complete this statement:

"When I can meet your need while staying connected to myself, I

feel _____ because _____."

Then share with your partner:

"Here's how you can support me as I try to meet your need: _____

_____."

## Share

Take turns discussing how to create a rhythm that honors both partners' needs. Ask each other:

"What helps you feel supported when I need space?"

"What helps me feel grounded when you need closeness?"

End by expressing appreciation for each other's willingness to find balance instead of blame.

**RelationTip:** Love doesn't mean losing yourself—it means showing up as yourself. When both partners can name what they need and what helps them give, the relationship becomes a safe space for two whole humans to keep choosing each other.

# Day 39: Asking for What You Need

Many of us were never taught how to ask for what we need. Instead, we hint, suppress, or hope our partner will pick up on the signs. But unspoken needs often turn into unmet needs—and unmet needs quietly erode connection over time.

*Unspoken + Unmet = Unfulfilled*

Asking clearly and kindly isn't a burden—it's a bridge. It invites your partner into your inner world and gives them the chance to love you in ways that actually make sense. When you ask directly, you're not being needy—you're being honest.

As Dr. Sue Johnson (2008) reminds us, expressing our needs openly and safely is one of the keys to emotional accessibility, responsiveness, and engagement—the foundation of secure love. Learning to voice your needs is how you build the trust that says, *"You matter to me, and I believe I matter to you."*

## Reflect

Think about a time you felt hesitant or afraid to ask for what you needed.
What held you back, and how did that impact your relationship?
What emotions came up when you stayed silent or hoped your partner would just know?

## Engage

Write down a need that you often hesitate to voice.

_____

_____

_____

## Prompt

Complete this statement:

"When I ask for _____, it helps me feel _____ and improves our relationship by _____."

**Example:**
"When I ask for a hug, it helps me feel loved and improves our relationship by helping me feel secure."

## Share

Take turns expressing one specific need you'd like to practice asking for more often.
After each share, ask:
"Was my request clear and kind?"
"How can I better communicate my needs to you in the future?"

**RelationTip:** Asking for what you need isn't demanding—it's inviting your partner into deeper connection, clarity, and care. Love grows when you stop expecting mind-reading and start practicing mutual understanding.

# Day 40: Beneath the Behavior

Behind every sharp tone, withdrawn moment, or overreaction is usually an unmet need. When we pause to look beneath the behavior—ours or our partner's—we often discover something softer: a longing for connection, reassurance, safety, or understanding.

As Dr. Sue Johnson (2008) reminds us, conflict is rarely about the surface issue; it's about the emotional signal underneath—the need to know, *"Are you there for me?"* Similarly, Dr. Marshall Rosenberg (2003) teaches that when we begin to see behavior as an expression of unmet needs rather than an attack or rejection, we transform conflict into connection.

When we focus on the need instead of the reaction, we move from judgment to compassion. We begin to see the hurt beneath the anger, the fear beneath the silence, and the longing beneath the frustration.

## Reflect

Think back to a recent conflict or moment of tension.
What might have been the true need beneath your reaction?
What might your partner have been longing for beneath theirs?

## Engage

Have an open conversation about a recent disagreement.
Each of you should try to identify what emotional need was present but unspoken during that moment. Listen without correcting—just notice what's underneath.

## Prompt

Complete this statement:

"When I reacted by _____, I was actually needing _____. Next time, I will work on communicating that need more clearly."

Example:
"When I reacted by getting loud, I was actually needing to feel heard. Next time, I'll work on communicating that more clearly."

## Share

Talk together about what shifts when you focus on needs instead of behaviors.

Ask:
"How might this awareness change how we approach conflict moving forward?"
"What does it feel like to see each other's needs instead of each other's flaws?"

**RelationTip:** Every behavior is a signal—a way of asking for something we need but may not know how to request. When we learn to listen for the need beneath the noise, compassion replaces confusion, and connection begins again.

# Day 41: Meeting Needs in Small, Everyday Ways

Meeting your partner's needs doesn't have to look like sweeping romantic gestures or big moments. More often, it's the quiet, consistent actions—a reassuring touch, a thoughtful text, a soft word at the right time—that do the most relational heavy lifting.

For me, it's her hand on my leg.
For Amber, it's me taking out the trash.

We experience our needs being met in vastly different ways, but both are effective. What matters isn't how big the act is—it's that love shows up in real, repeatable ways. As Dr. John Gottman (2011) found, relationships thrive not through grand gestures but through "small things often." These everyday moments of connection are what sustain love and safety over time.

Today's focus is on finding those small, meaningful actions that keep your connection strong day after day.

## Reflect

Think about how small, everyday efforts could make your partner feel more supported.
How might those gestures build trust, warmth, and connection over time?
What little things make you feel seen and cared for?

## Engage

Ask your partner for one small thing you can do frequently to help meet their needs. Then reflect on your own—what's one small way they could do the same for you?

## Prompt

Complete this together: "I will try to meet your need for

_____ by _____.

## Share

Talk through how you'd like to be reminded or thanked when your need is being met. Reinforcing the habit of noticing and appreciating these small efforts helps the rhythm stick and keeps your relationship fueled by gratitude instead of assumption.

**RelationTip:** Grand gestures might make movies, but daily attentiveness builds marriages. It's the little things—done with love, done again and again—that create safety, trust, and connection that lasts.

# Day 42: Creating a Needs Action Plan

This week has been about more than identifying needs—it's been about rediscovering your humanity through them. Needs don't make us weak; they make us reachable.

When we stop hiding what we long for and start sharing it with honesty and tenderness, our relationships become places of safety instead of shame. Building a relationship that welcomes needs is how we build a love that lasts.

As Dr. Sue Johnson (2008) reminds us, emotional responsiveness—tuning in to each other's needs and fears—is what transforms ordinary relationships into secure bonds. It's not about perfect attunement; it's about consistent care—the daily practice of saying, *"I see you. I hear you. I want to meet you where you are."*

Today is your chance to turn awareness into rhythm—not just to name your needs, but to nurture them.

## Reflect

Think back on what you've learned about needs this week.
How have your perspectives shifted?
What did you learn about your own needs—and your partner's?

## Engage

Together, create a simple "Needs Action Plan."
Each of you should name your top three emotional needs and discuss practical, everyday ways to support one another in meeting them. Think small, repeatable, and specific—things that quietly say, *"I'm paying attention."* This isn't about perfection; it's about intention.

## Prompt

Complete this statement together:

"Moving forward, we will support each other's needs by _____
_____."

## Share

Take a moment to affirm each other's needs—not as burdens, but as beautiful reminders that you're both human and worthy of care. Let this be a reset—a recommitment to showing up intentionally and consistently. Hold hands. Breathe together. Say thank you.

**RelationTip:** You are allowed to have needs. You are allowed to meet them. And you are absolutely allowed to ask for help. True love doesn't erase need; it responds to it with grace.

# WEEK 7

# TOGETHER,
# BUT NOT THE SAME

# Week 7: Together, But Not the Same

*Secure connection is built on two grounding truths:*
*We belong to each other.*
*And we are still our own.*

Healthy love doesn't ask us to lose ourselves—it invites us to bring our whole selves forward. When we honor individuality, we protect the space where curiosity, creativity, and freedom can thrive. It's not about choosing between *me* or *we*—it's about learning how both can coexist beautifully.

I've learned this the hard way in my own marriage. Amber and I couldn't be more different. I'm the talker; she's the thinker. I want to process right away; she needs time to breathe. I thrive on ideas; she finds peace in quiet. Early in our relationship, I mistook those differences for distance. I thought sameness was the goal—that harmony meant agreement.

But over time, I began to see that our differences were actually the strength of our bond. When we stopped trying to make each other the same—and started seeing our individuality as a gift—our relationship began to breathe again.

That's what this week is about: learning to stay deeply connected without losing yourself.

Research supports what love has been teaching us all along. Studies show that couples who honor each other's individuality experience greater intimacy, higher satisfaction, and more trust (Schnarch, 1997; Lerner, 2005). When both partners have room to be themselves, the relationship becomes more resilient, more alive, and far less reactive.

Family therapist Murray Bowen (1978) called this *differentiation*— the ability to stay connected while staying true to who you are. Differentiation is what allows you to say, "I can hold my ground without pulling away." It's the balance between closeness and autonomy—between "I need you" and "I know me."

When couples lose sight of their individuality, they risk becoming enmeshed—blurring emotional boundaries and depending too heavily on each other for identity, validation, or stability. Over time, that over-reliance can quietly create exhaustion, resentment, or even disconnection. As Bowen's research shows, healthy differentiation helps partners navigate differences without fear, engage conflict with curiosity, and support one another's growth without needing to control it (Bowen, 1978; Kerr & Bowen, 1988).

Here are four ways to practice individuality while staying deeply connected:

1. **Create Personal Space and Time**
   Regularly engage in individual hobbies, friendships, or self-care activities. Maintaining personal space allows each partner to recharge and bring fresh energy and stories into the relationship.

2. **Encourage Personal Growth**
   Support each other's goals and dreams. Recognize that your partner's growth can enhance—not threaten—the relationship.

3. **Communicate Needs Openly**
   Talk honestly about individual needs and boundaries. Respecting these differences builds trust and mutual respect.

4. **Differentiate Emotional Responses**
   Practice self-regulation before seeking reassurance. When you can calm yourself, you show up with strength, not reactivity.

When we honor individuality, we invite freedom, admiration, and maturity into love. Togetherness isn't about sameness—it's about standing side by side as two whole people who keep choosing each other, again and again.

When we allow space for difference, we make room for discovery. And it's in that space—where freedom meets belonging—that love finally exhales.

Let's dig into Day 43 and begin this week's work.

# Day 43: Embracing Differences

What makes you different from your partner isn't a problem to solve—it's an opportunity to understand each other more fully.

Healthy connection doesn't require sameness. Your partner was a whole person long before your relationship began—with their own history, preferences, rhythms, and ways of moving through the world. It's easy to assume that closeness means blending, matching, or mirroring. But the truth is, the strongest relationships hold space for two full selves—not half-sized versions of each person.

As Amber and I have learned, supporting each other's individuality doesn't pull us apart; it strengthens our trust. We sometimes travel separately. We think differently, process emotions differently, and even rest differently. Yet our bond has grown deeper because we honor what makes each other unique instead of trying to make each other the same.

As Dr. David Schnarch (1997) reminds us, differentiation—staying connected while maintaining your individuality—is what allows intimacy to flourish without fusion. When each partner remains grounded in who they are, the relationship has more room to breathe, grow, and expand.

This is a partnership, not a merger.

In a merger, differences get swallowed, blurred, or absorbed for the sake of harmony. But in a partnership, individuality is respected, protected, and even celebrated. You don't have to agree on everything, share the same hobbies, or make identical choices to build a beautiful life together. What matters is the commitment to remain connected *while* allowing each other to be fully yourselves.

When you treat your differences not as threats but as invitations—to learn, to listen, to stretch—you build a kind of intimacy that feels both spacious and secure.

## Reflect

Take a few moments to think about your partner as an individual. Ask yourself: What makes them "them"? What passions or dreams do they carry that aren't about us—but just about them? How do they express themselves differently than I do? Have I always supported that, or have I resisted it in some way?

## Engage

Write down three things you know to be unique about your partner.

1. _____

2. _____

3. _____

## Prompt

"I can be more supportive of your individuality by _____
_____."

## Share

Have a conversation about how you can each feel safe to grow as individuals while staying rooted as a couple.

**RelationTip:** A secure relationship isn't threatened by autonomy—it's strengthened by it. The more freedom we feel to be ourselves, the more joy, energy, and creativity we bring back to one another.

# Day 44: Supporting Personal Growth

Supporting each other's growth is one of the most powerful ways to strengthen your bond. Love deepens when both partners are free to evolve—to learn, explore, and become more of who they're meant to be. When you celebrate your partner's unfolding story, you send a sacred message: *"I love all of you—even the parts still becoming."*

In our own marriage, Amber and I learned that growth can be confusing at first. When one of us changed in ways the other didn't expect, it sometimes felt like distance. But over time we realized something important: the discomfort wasn't a sign that we were growing apart—it was a sign that we were growing. When we leaned into curiosity instead of fear, those seasons of change became the very moments that strengthened our connection.

Research echoes this experience. Dr. John Gottman reminds us that nurturing our passions and identity outside the relationship supports autonomy, fulfillment, and long-term satisfaction (Gottman & Silver, 2015). Personal growth doesn't compete with love—it fuels it. When each partner feels free to pursue purpose and joy, the relationship stays alive, vibrant, and connected to something larger than itself.

Healthy couples learn this rhythm of freedom and belonging. They say:
"Go do you."
"Come back to us."

That's the dance of trust—two people walking side by side, growing in parallel, cheering for each other as they go.

## Reflect

Think of a dream, goal, or personal interest your partner has that you haven't fully known how to support—or maybe have a hard time understanding.

## Engage

Write down how you might be of more support in this area.

_____

_____

_____

## Prompt

"One way I could better support your personal growth this week is by _____ because I know it helps you feel _____."

## Share

End by affirming what you see in your partner: "I believe in your dreams, and I'm here for the journey." You don't have to understand everything to stand beside it—you just have to keep showing up, again and again.

**RelationTip:** A thriving relationship doesn't ask your partner to shrink—it creates space for them to expand. When you celebrate who they're becoming, love keeps growing too.

# Day 45: Boundaries and Autonomy

Boundaries are one of the most misunderstood parts of a healthy relationship. Many people hear the word and immediately think of walls, distance, or selfishness. But in reality, boundaries are the opposite of disconnection — they're what allow two people to stay close *without losing themselves.*

Healthy boundaries protect your well-being, clarify your needs, and create space for each partner's individuality to thrive. They're not demands or punishments; they're expressions of clarity, self-respect, and emotional responsibility.

In our culture, we often confuse love with fusion — the idea that if two people are "really close," they should think alike, want the same things, and need each other in identical ways. But that's not intimacy. That's sameness. Real intimacy requires room to breathe.

Esther Perel says it this way: "Love rests on two pillars: surrender and autonomy." Those two forces — togetherness and individuality — are constantly dancing in every long-term partnership. When they're balanced, connection feels alive, energized, and secure.

As Harriet Lerner writes, *"The most basic boundary-setting word is 'no.' It lets others know that we exist apart from them."* A relationship becomes healthier — not colder — when both partners have permission to be fully themselves. A strong "no" often protects the integrity of a deeply trustworthy "yes."

Boundaries aren't about creating distance; they're about creating clarity. They let your partner know how to love you in ways that feel safe, respectful, and sustainable.

**So what do healthy boundaries actually look like in a relationship?**

Here are a few examples that help partners stay connected *without* collapsing into each other:

1.  **Emotional Boundaries**
    "I need time to process before we keep talking. I'm not leaving — I just want to respond thoughtfully."

2.  **Time Boundaries**
    "I want to spend time together tonight, but I also need 30 minutes to decompress after work."

3.  **Digital Boundaries**
    "Let's both agree not to bring our phones to bed so we can be more present with each other."

4.  **Personal Boundaries**
    "I love you, and I also need creative time each week that's just for me."

5.  **Conflict Boundaries**
    "If things get heated, can we agree to take a pause and return when we're calmer?"

These kinds of boundaries aren't barriers to closeness — they're the building blocks of emotional safety. Sue Johnson reminds us that secure relationships depend on clear signals, predictable patterns, and the ability to stay connected *while* honoring differences and limits. Boundaries make that possible because they help partners navigate needs with clarity instead of confusion.

Boundaries are not about separation. They're about structure — the kind of structure that lets intimacy deepen rather than collapse under pressure.

## Reflect

How does the word *boundaries* make you feel? Does that word sound freeing — or does it bring up discomfort, fear, or guilt?

## Engage

Write down one belief you've carried about boundaries — whether helpful or unhelpful — and where you think it came from.

_____

_____

_____

## Prompt

Complete this sentence: **"A boundary that would help me feel more connected and grounded in our relationship is _____**

**_____."**

## Share

Take turns explaining why that boundary matters to you. Focus on clarity, not blame. Remember: boundaries are invitations for connection, not punishments. And listen to your partner's boundary as an act of respect, not threat.

**RelationTip:** Boundaries don't push love away; they guide it. When you honor your limits and your partner's, you create a relationship where individuality isn't feared — it's cherished.

> *"Boundaries are the distance at which*
> *I can love you and me simultaneously."*
> **— Prentis Hemphill**

# Day 46: Recognizing Support

Healthy love isn't measured by how much time you spend together—it's measured by how safe you feel to grow, explore, and still know you're supported. In a secure relationship, support doesn't mean control or constant involvement. It means trust—the quiet confidence that your partner is with you, even when you're walking your own path.

Support sounds like:
"I see you."
"I believe in you."
"I'm here when you need me."

True support doesn't rescue, fix, or steer. It witnesses. It's choosing to stand beside your partner, not above them. It's cheering for their individuality without trying to shape it.

Often, the most meaningful expressions of support aren't grand gestures, but small, steady ones—the encouraging text before a big day, the hand on the shoulder before a risk, the quiet "You've got this" when doubt creeps in. Those moments whisper, *I see you, and I'm proud of you.*

Dr. Sue Johnson (2008) describes this as creating a secure base—a relationship where both partners feel safe enough to explore, risk, and grow, knowing they can always return to love.

## Reflect

Think of a few times when your partner supported your individuality—maybe they encouraged you to take a risk, pursue a dream, or gave you space to grow.

## Engage

Write down one of those times that stands out, and then use the prompt below to continue the conversation.

_____

_____

_____

## Prompt

"When you supported me in _____, I felt
_____. That kind of support made me feel closer to
you."

## Share

Take turns expressing gratitude for how you've supported one another's growth and individuality.

End with a simple affirmation: *"I see how far you've come, and I'm proud of you."*

Notice how it feels to say that—and to hear it.

**RelationTip:** Support doesn't always mean doing or fixing. Sometimes it means simply standing beside your partner, hand on their back, whispering, *"Go for it. I've got you."*

# Day 47: Balancing Autonomy and Connection

Healthy love lives in the tension between *me* and *we*. Too much togetherness can feel suffocating; too much space can feel like distance. The balance between autonomy and connection isn't something you find once—it's something you continually adjust as life, seasons, and needs change.

When both partners feel free to grow, pursue passions, and still stay emotionally connected, the relationship becomes a place of freedom rather than confinement. The goal isn't perfect balance—it's awareness, curiosity, and care.

Dr. Sue Johnson (2008) reminds us that secure relationships are flexible relationships. Emotional safety allows you to move naturally between closeness and independence without fear of abandonment or loss. It's what makes it possible to say, "I'm here with you," while also saying, "I trust you as you grow."

To make this balance feel practical and grounded, here are a few gentle ways to weave autonomy *and* connection into daily life:

1. **Maintain personal hobbies—and share them when it fits.**
   Example: You might love hiking as a way to recharge. Invite your partner sometimes, but also honor the solo hikes that ground you. This lets you share parts of your world without losing independence.

2. **Communicate your need for space with love.**
   Example: After a long day you might say, "I just need a few minutes to clear my head, and then I want to be fully present with you." This helps your partner feel included rather than shut out.

3. **Be transparent about your individuality.**
   Example: "I've been wanting to try this workshop—it's something just for me, but I'd love to tell you about it afterward." Openness builds trust and keeps curiosity alive.

## Reflect

Take a moment to consider how you've navigated autonomy and togetherness in your relationship.

- Do you feel free to grow as an individual?
- Does your partner feel supported in their own growth?

## Engage

Write down what a healthy balance between your autonomy and your relationship looks like for you.

_____

_____

_____

## Prompt

"For me, balance looks like _____. It helps me feel _____, and I believe it strengthens our connection because _____."

## Share

Take turns sharing what you wrote. Then come up with one or two small ways to nurture that balance this week—maybe scheduling solo time, revisiting a shared hobby, or having a weekly check-in.

End with this affirmation: **"I want us both to feel free and connected—not one or the other, but both."**

**RelationTip:** You don't have to choose between *me* and *we*. The healthiest relationships make room for both. When each partner feels safe to be fully themselves and fully connected, love stops being a tug-of-war and becomes a dance.

# Day 48: Celebrating Each Other's Strengths

Every relationship is made stronger by the unique strengths each partner brings. Maybe your partner is steady when you're overwhelmed. Maybe they're the dreamer when you're the planner. Maybe they bring humor, wisdom, patience, creativity, or courage into your shared life. These strengths don't just shape who they are—they shape the relationship you're building together.

When you learn to notice and name these strengths, something powerful happens: your partner feels seen not just for what they contribute, but for who they are at their core. Affirming each other's strengths transforms everyday interactions into moments of connection, grounding your relationship in appreciation rather than criticism.

Drs. John and Julie Gottman (2017) found that thriving couples intentionally build a "culture of appreciation"—a way of relating where partners regularly name and celebrate each other's positive qualities. This practice creates emotional safety, deepens trust, and strengthens the bond over time. When you actively notice your partner's strengths, you shift the entire emotional climate of your relationship.

## Reflect

Think about the top three to five strengths you admire most in your partner. These could be big—like resilience, empathy, or leadership—or small—like the way they make coffee just how you like it.

## Engage

Write down those top three to five strengths below.

1. _____

2. _____

3. _____

4. _____

5. _____

## Prompt

"The strength I find most attractive about you is _____, because when you show it, I feel _____."

## Share

Take turns sharing your lists with each other. Go slow. Look them in the eyes as you say each quality out loud. Let the words sink in.

**RelationTip:** Love grows stronger when we name what's good. The more we celebrate each other's strengths, the more we create a relationship grounded not just in fixing problems, but in nurturing what's already beautiful.

# Day 49: Reflecting on the Week's Progress

Honoring individuality isn't something you check off a list — it's a lifelong rhythm.

Healthy relationships breathe. They expand and contract as both partners grow, change, and rediscover themselves.

When you give each other the freedom to explore, to rest, to dream, and to return, you create the kind of safety that says: *"You can be fully you, and we will still be us."*

Supporting your partner's autonomy doesn't mean drifting apart; it means trusting that love can stretch — that you can both evolve and still choose each other again and again.

The goal isn't to stay the same. It's to stay connected while you keep becoming.

Continue to celebrate each other's growth, even when it looks different from your own. That difference isn't disconnection — it's diversity. And when honored, it becomes one of the deepest sources of intimacy.

As Dr. David Schnarch (1997) teaches, differentiation allows two people to "stand on their own two feet and still embrace each other." And Sue Johnson (2008) reminds us that secure connection thrives when love creates both *freedom and safety.*

## Reflect

Think about what you've learned this week about your partner's individuality.

## Engage

Write the most surprising or significant insight from this week about your partner.

_____

_____

_____

## Prompt

"One thing I can keep doing to honor your individuality is _____

_____."

## Share

Speak this one simple commitment to continue supporting each other's journey: "I love who you are, and I'm excited to keep discovering who you're becoming."

**RelationTip:** When you both feel safe to grow, you don't outgrow each other — you grow together.

# WEEK 8

# CLOSER THAN WORDS

# Week 8: Closer Than Words

Last week, you explored individuality — the art of being you without losing *us*.

Now, we turn toward what happens when two whole people draw near again: intimacy.

Intimacy isn't just closeness — it's safety, vulnerability, and presence. It's the quiet knowing that your partner truly sees you — not the polished or curated version, but the unguarded one — and still chooses to stay. It's that sacred moment that whispers: "I see you. I hear you. I'm here."

After learning to hold your individuality, intimacy is the gentle return — the movement back toward "us." It's where curiosity replaces assumption and where love becomes less about performance and more about presence.

Contrary to popular belief, intimacy isn't just physical. While holding hands, sharing a kiss, or making love can deepen connection, real intimacy is also found in the spaces words can't fill — a shared laugh, a lingering glance, an honest apology, or the quiet comfort of sitting in silence after a long day.

In thriving relationships, intimacy shows up in many forms: emotional, physical, intellectual, spiritual, creative, and even playful. It's how we say, in countless ways, "I choose you again."

But intimacy doesn't just happen. It requires time, curiosity, and intention. It asks us to pause — to reach across the couch, the bed, the silence — and remind each other that we're still here. In seasons when stress, parenting, or routine pull you apart, these small, intentional moments of closeness become the stitches that hold your relationship together.

When we nurture intimacy, we're not just maintaining connection — we're deepening trust. We're building the kind of safety that makes love sustainable through both the storms and the stillness.

This week, you'll explore what intimacy means in your relationship:

- Where do you feel most connected?
- Where do you long for more closeness?
- And how can you gently invite each other into deeper presence?

There's no formula for intimacy. The goal isn't to perfect it — it's to practice it. Love grows in the steady return to each other — one moment, one conversation, one breath at a time.

To get us started, I want to share five ways to nurture intimacy. These five qualities will show up in various ways in your work this week.

1. **Create intentional time together.**
   Set aside distraction-free moments to connect — even ten minutes of undivided attention can strengthen emotional closeness.

2. **Share your inner world.**
   Talk about feelings, hopes, and fears — not just logistics. Let your partner in on what's happening inside you.

3. **Practice small acts of affection.**
   A gentle touch, lingering eye contact, or a note of appreciation all remind your partner, "I see you."

4. **Listen with empathy.**
   Don't fix — just understand. Empathy transforms tension into tenderness.

5. **Be curious, not critical.**
   Ask open-ended questions about your partner's experiences and dreams. Curiosity says, "You still matter to me."

Let's begin this week by defining what intimacy means to you — and how you can keep choosing it, day after day.

# Day 50: Defining Intimacy

As Pia Mellody teaches, true intimacy isn't about merging — it's about meeting each other's truth with openness and without demand.

Last week was about honoring individuality — learning that love doesn't mean losing yourself.
This week asks the next question: What happens when two whole people come close again?

Intimacy is the art of knowing and being known. It's the slow unfolding of truth — showing your inner world and allowing your partner to meet you there. The look across the table that says, *I'm with you, even when words fall short.*

For some, intimacy means physical closeness. For others, it's emotional vulnerability, spiritual connection, shared laughter, or simply the safety of being seen without needing to perform.
Whatever it looks like, intimacy always grows in the same soil — honesty, curiosity, and safety.

Today's exercise helps you both explore what intimacy means to you and how you can keep inviting each other closer — without losing yourselves in the process.

## Reflect

Take a few quiet moments to answer for yourself:

- When do I feel most intimate with my partner?
- How do I express intimacy?
- How do I prefer intimacy to be expressed toward me?

## Engage

Turn and share your reflections with your partner. Approach the conversation with curiosity, not correction. Practice listening with your whole presence — no fixing, no defending, just receiving. Use the prompt below if you need help getting started.

## Prompt

"I feel emotionally closest to you when _____."
Let your partner's response teach you something new — even if you've known them for decades.

## Share

Create a shared definition of intimacy together. Write or say what intimacy means to *us* — what it feels like, looks like, and how you'll nurture it in this season of your relationship.

Example: "For us, intimacy means slowing down, being honest about what we feel, and staying soft even when we're tired."

Then, read your definition aloud and notice how it feels to speak it into the room — to name what you both long for.

_____

_____

_____

## RelationTip:

Intimacy = *Into-Me-See.*
Letting someone truly see you — unfiltered, unmasked, unafraid
— is one of the bravest and most connecting things you can do.
The more we show up as we are, the more we invite our partner to
do the same.

# Day 51: Barriers to Intimacy

Sometimes the hardest part of intimacy isn't desire or love — it's the barriers we have in place or the ones we create out of fear.

Fear of rejection.
Fear of being too much.
Fear that if we show our true selves, the other person might not stay.

Every couple encounters barriers to intimacy. They can be as subtle as distraction or busyness, or as deep as shame, unresolved hurt, or old attachment wounds that whisper, *"Don't get too close — it's safer that way."*

Dr. Sue Johnson (2008) reminds us that "we are wired for connection, but trauma and disconnection teach us to protect instead of reach."

When we protect, we pull back — even from the people who love us most. Brené Brown (2012) teaches that vulnerability is the birthplace of connection, yet it's also where fear shows up first. And when fear rises, the brain often shifts into protection mode rather than openness — something Dr. Dan Siegel (2012) notes happens when our nervous systems sense emotional threat.

Today's exercise helps you notice those protective patterns, not to judge them, but to understand what they're trying to guard. Awareness opens the door for compassion — and compassion is what begins to melt those barriers.

## Reflect

Think about what sometimes makes closeness hard for you.

- What do you fear might happen if you let your partner see more of your inner world?

- What emotions (shame, sadness, anger, fear) tend to close you off?

## Engage

Write down one or two barriers to intimacy that pop up for you from time to time.

_____

_____

_____

## Prompt

"One thing that makes intimacy hard for me at times is _____, and when that happens, what I most need from you is _____."

## Share

After both of you have shared, talk about what compassion might look like in those moments. How can you remind each other that it's safe to come close again? End with a gentle affirmation such as: "Even when it's hard to open up, I want you to know I'm still here — and I'm trying."

**RelationTip:** Barriers don't mean something's broken — they're often signs that something inside you needs care. When you approach each other's walls with curiosity instead of frustration, you don't just lower defenses; you build trust.

# Day 52: Remembering Special Moments

Sometimes, the best way to move toward deeper intimacy is to remember when you've already been there.

After exploring what can block closeness, today is about returning to the moments that remind you what connection really feels like — the laughter that softened tension, the quiet comfort after a hard day, the gaze that said, *"You're safe with me."*

These memories aren't just sentimental; they're sacred. They hold the blueprint of what your relationship looks and feels like when its most alive. When you revisit them together, you remind your nervous systems that safety, warmth, and closeness are possible — because you've already lived them. As Dr. Dan Siegel (2012) describes, shared emotional experiences strengthen the integration between body, brain, and relationship, helping us feel more connected and secure.

Dr. Sue Johnson (2008) echoes this truth in her work on attachment: when couples recall moments of emotional bonding, they re-activate the neural pathways of safety and love, which helps repair distance and deepen trust.

## Reflect

Think back to a time you felt completely connected with your partner.

- What made that moment feel meaningful?
- Was it emotional vulnerability, laughter, physical closeness, or shared stillness?
- How did your body feel — calm, grounded, open, alive?

## Engage

Share your memory with your partner. Focus on the emotion, not just the story. As you speak, notice their reaction — sometimes, hearing how a moment landed for the other person reveals something new and healing. Use the prompt below if you need help getting started.

## Prompt

"I felt closest to you when we _____.

That moment made me feel _____

because _____."

Then add:

"Something we could do to create a similar experience again is ___

_____."

## Share

Discuss how you might intentionally create more of these moments in your current season of life. What helps you both feel seen, safe, and close?

End with a simple act of connection — a hug, a kiss, or holding hands — whatever helps your bodies remember the feeling of togetherness.

**RelationTip:** Intimacy doesn't always need to be invented — sometimes it just needs to be remembered. The moments that made you feel close before can guide you back home to each other again and again.

# Day 53: Practicing Vulnerability

*"Vulnerability is the birthplace of love, belonging, joy, courage, empathy, and creativity."*
**— Brené Brown (2012)**

Yesterday, you reflected on moments when you felt close and safe with your partner.

Today is about creating those moments again — not by recreating the past, but by opening your heart in the present.

Vulnerability is the heartbeat of intimacy — it's how love breathes. It's the quiet courage of saying, "Here's where I'm tender," and trusting that the person across from you will stay.

When you share your fears, hopes, or hidden insecurities, you're inviting your partner into your inner world — the place where connection lives. And when that openness is met with warmth and acceptance, safety expands, trust deepens, and intimacy takes root.

As Dr. Sue Johnson (2008) explains, when partners risk emotional openness and are met with attuned responsiveness, it literally rewires the brain for greater trust and emotional security. Vulnerability transforms isolation into intimacy.

True connection doesn't come from perfection — it comes from presence.
Every time you open your heart and your partner meets you with empathy, your relationship becomes a safer, softer place to land.

Here are a few ways couples practice vulnerability together:

1. **Expressing fears and insecurities.**
   One partner opens up about a worry or feeling of inadequacy

— the other listens with empathy, not solutions. Sharing fears out loud reduces their power.

2. **Sharing past pain.**
   Confiding in one another about painful experiences builds compassion. When your partner hears your story with gentleness, healing begins to unfold.

3. **Asking for reassurance.**
   It's okay to need comfort. Saying, "I need to know you still choose me," or "I'm feeling insecure right now," helps bridge emotional distance rather than widen it.

## Reflect

Think about what it's like for you to share your deepest fears, desires, or needs.

- What holds you back from opening up?

- What would it mean to feel fully seen — without fear of rejection?

- What do you long for your partner to understand or hold gently?

## Engage

Take a breath. Then share one thing vulnerable with your partner — a fear, a desire, or a boundary. You might feel nervous, but that's part of the courage it takes to connect.
Remember: vulnerability isn't weakness — it's an act of strength and trust.

## Prompt

"Sharing this with you made me feel _____.
What I need from you in this space is _____."

## Share

Talk together about what it felt like to be open.
Were there moments of discomfort? Relief? Gratitude?

How did it feel to be trusted with your partner's truth?
End with something grounding — a hand on their arm, a long hug, a simple "thank you." Let your bodies remember safety.

**RelationTip:** Vulnerability is the doorway to intimacy. Each time you risk being real, you teach each other that love can hold the weight of your truth.

# Day 54: Emotional Intimacy in Action

Emotional intimacy grows quietly — in the pauses, the glances, the ordinary rhythms of being together. It lives in your tone when you say good morning. It hides in the way you listen, reach for their hand, or soften your voice when tension rises. It's less about candlelight and more about consistency — the quiet, daily ways you remind your partner: *"I'm here. You can count on me."*

True intimacy is lived, not just spoken. It's the act of turning toward your partner — again and again — especially when it would be easier to turn away. Dr. John Gottman (2015) calls this the foundation of trust: responding to your partner's "bids for connection," those small moments when they reach out, even subtly, for reassurance or closeness.

When you choose to respond — to notice, to stay present, to engage — you turn an ordinary moment into an intimate one.

## Reflect

Think about your everyday interactions.

- When does your partner tend to reach out for connection (in words, looks, or gestures)?
- How do you usually respond — do you notice, or sometimes miss it?
- What would it look like to respond with more warmth and intention this week?

## Engage

Spend today looking for small bids for connection — a sigh, a smile, a question, or even a complaint that might be masking a longing for closeness. When you notice one, try responding differently. Turn toward. Offer your presence instead of a solution. Sometimes, the most intimate words are, "I'm listening," or, "That sounds hard — I'm here."

## Prompt

"One way I can turn toward you more this week_____.
When you reach for me — even in small ways — I want to _____."

## Share

At the end of the day, talk about how it felt to practice emotional intimacy in these small moments.

What did you notice in your partner's reactions? In your own?

End your conversation with this gentle affirmation: "Every time I choose connection, I'm choosing us."

**RelationTip:** Intimacy doesn't need perfect timing — it needs presence. The more often you turn toward each other in small ways, the stronger your love becomes in the big ones.

# Day 55: Physical Intimacy and Presence

Physical intimacy is one of the most powerful ways we communicate safety, love, and belonging — often without saying a word. It's not only about sex; it's about presence. A soft touch on the arm. A warm hug after a long day. Sitting shoulder-to-shoulder in quiet connection.

When physical intimacy flows from emotional safety, it becomes an expression of love rather than obligation. It says: *"You're safe here. You matter. I choose you."*

But when stress, distance, or disconnection enter the picture, physical closeness can feel complicated — even loaded. One partner might crave touch while the other pulls away, not from lack of love, but from fear of pressure or rejection. Rebuilding trust around touch means starting small and staying attuned to each other's comfort levels.

As Dr. Sue Johnson (2013) writes, "Loving touch is a potent way to send the message 'You are not alone.' It's the language of connection when words fall short."

Today is about slowing down and rediscovering that language together — gently, with curiosity and care.

## Reflect

Take a moment to consider your current physical connection.

- What does physical affection look like in your relationship right now?
- Do you feel comfortable initiating or receiving touch?
- Are there moments when you long for closeness but hesitate to reach out?

## Engage

Spend time practicing non-sexual physical connection today.
Hold hands during a walk. Sit together in silence. Hug longer than usual. Touch without agenda — just presence.
Pay attention to what happens in your body as you connect.
Do you feel your shoulders relax? Your breath slow?
That's your nervous system recognizing safety.

## Prompt

"When you touch me, I feel _____.

What helps me feel more connected through touch is _____."

## Share

Talk together about how you each experience physical closeness. What feels connecting? What sometimes feels pressured or missed? Remember — physical intimacy deepens when both partners feel free, not forced. End your conversation by expressing gratitude for one another's openness and willingness to connect.

**RelationTip:** Physical intimacy is not about performance; it's about presence. When touch becomes a way of saying "I'm here with you" — it moves from routine to sacred.

# Day 56: Reflecting on Your Intimacy Journey

Intimacy isn't a destination — it's a rhythm.
A steady dance of reaching, retreating, and returning.
It lives in the courage to be known, the grace to stay curious, and the quiet trust that whispers, "We're safe here."

This week has been about exploring what closeness really means — how emotion, affection, and presence weave together to create connection. You've practiced honesty, vulnerability, and touch. You've taken time to notice what helps love feel near — and what makes it feel far away.

As you reflect on your journey this week, remember: intimacy doesn't require perfection — it asks for intention. The more often you show up with openness and care, the safer and stronger your love becomes.

## Reflect

What new insights have you gained about intimacy this week?

## Engage

What's one major takeaway from this week's work that has impacted you most? Write that down here:

_____

_____

_____

## Prompt

"What I've learned about intimacy this week is _____.
One way I want to keep growing in this area is _____."

## Share

Take turns sharing your reflections.

Then, together, name one simple ritual that helps you stay close — a weekly walk, a morning check-in, or a nightly hug before bed.

Commit to practicing that rhythm of connection in the days ahead.

**RelationTip:** Intimacy isn't about discovering something new — it's about returning, again and again, to what's already between you, with tenderness, curiosity, and courage.

# WEEK 9

# THE COURAGE TO BEGIN AGAIN

# Week 9: The Courage to Begin Again

*"Forgiveness is giving up the hope that the past could have been any different."*
— **Oprah Winfrey (2010)**

That truth captures what research continues to affirm: forgiveness is not about forgetting or excusing — it's about emotional release and restoration. Studies show that practicing forgiveness improves relationship satisfaction, reduces stress, and strengthens both emotional and physical well-being (Worthington, 2006; Enright & Fitzgibbons, 2015).

Every couple who loves deeply will, at some point, also hurt deeply. Love makes us vulnerable — and vulnerability means we will sometimes miss, misunderstand, or wound each other. The health of a relationship isn't measured by the absence of hurt but by your capacity to repair it (Johnson, 2008).

This week is about courage — the courage to turn toward one another again, even when it would be easier to turn away.

Forgiveness isn't pretending things are fine or sweeping pain under the rug. It's naming what was broken, grieving what was lost, and choosing a new path forward. It's less about erasing the past and more about deciding it won't define your future.

In our marriage, Amber and I have faced moments that stretched us to our limits — times when silence felt safer than honesty, when fear spoke louder than love. What saved us wasn't perfection; it was the steady willingness to return. To try again. To begin again.

That's what forgiveness really is: a new beginning.

Forgiveness asks for tenderness. It balances truth with compassion, accountability with grace. It sounds like, "This hurt me," and also, "I still want to build something beautiful with you."

This week, we'll use the **HEART Model™** as a gentle guide to move from hurt toward healing:

**H – Honor the Hurt:** Name what was painful without minimizing or rushing past it.
**E – Empathize with the Experience:** Try to understand what was happening inside both of you — not to excuse, but to see clearly.
**A – Acknowledge Responsibility:** Take ownership where needed, and express what you needed instead of blame.
**R – Release the Resentment:** Choose to stop rehearsing the story of hurt. Begin loosening its grip.
**T – Turn Toward Repair:** Ask, "What can we do differently now?" and take one small step toward reconnection.

The HEART Model™ was developed through my clinical and personal work with couples as a simple, research-informed process for rebuilding trust and emotional safety.

## A Note on the HEART Model™

The HEART Model™ is designed to guide couples through everyday relational ruptures — moments of misunderstanding, emotional distance, or disappointment that occur in safe, non-abusive relationships. It is *not* intended to replace trauma work or address major violations such as infidelity, abuse, or betrayal trauma. In those cases, healing requires additional safety, time, and professional support before forgiveness can meaningfully begin. The HEART Model™ process can complement that deeper work when you're ready, but it should never rush it. True repair always honors both the injury *and* the pace of healing.

Forgiveness is not weakness — it's strength. It's the quiet bravery of opening your heart again after it's been bruised.

If trauma or abuse is part of your story, know that forgiveness is never about tolerating harm or reconciling too soon. Healing may require distance, therapy, or safety before forgiveness can unfold — and that's okay. True forgiveness isn't forced; it comes in its own time (Brown, 2012).

As you move through this week, remember forgiveness isn't something you *achieve* — it's something you *practice*. Each act of empathy, truth-telling, and grace becomes a step toward rebuilding trust.

Because love — real love — isn't the absence of hurt.
It's the presence of repair.

**RelationTip:** Forgiveness doesn't mean the wound never happened. It means you've chosen to stop letting it run the show. Healing begins when two people refuse to give up on the story they're still writing.

# Day 57: Honor the Hurt

Forgiveness is one of the bravest things you'll ever do in love. It's not about pretending the hurt didn't happen — it's about acknowledging the pain, honoring your story, and choosing to move toward healing. Forgiveness doesn't excuse what happened; it transforms what it did to you (Brown, 2012).

This work takes courage. It takes regulation. And it takes both partners showing up with softness.

As you begin, remember: your nervous system might have its own response to revisiting pain — tightening, shutting down, or wanting to flee. That's normal. Pause when needed. Breathe. Name what's happening. The goal isn't to rush forgiveness; it's to stay present with what's real (Johnson, 2008).

This week, we'll use the **HEART Model**™ that I developed as a gentle framework for healing through forgiveness:

**H – Honor the Hurt:** Name what was painful without minimizing or rushing past it.

**E – Empathize with the Experience:** Try to understand what was happening inside both of you in that moment — not to excuse it, but to see it more clearly.

**A – Acknowledge Responsibility:** Take ownership where needed, or name what you needed instead.

**R – Release the Resentment:** Choose to stop rehearsing the story of hurt. Let it start loosening its grip.

**T – Turn Toward Repair:** Ask, *"What can we do differently now?"* and take one small step toward reconnection.

Forgiveness is rarely instant — it unfolds in layers. What matters most is your willingness to begin.

## Reflect

Think about a time when you experienced hurt in your relationship — a moment of disappointment, misunderstanding, or betrayal.

Ask yourself:

- What made this experience painful for me?
- What emotions still linger when I recall it?
- What would healing look like, even if full forgiveness isn't possible yet?

## Engage

Invite your partner into a grounded, safe conversation about this hurt.

You might begin with: *"There's something I've held onto for a while, and I'd like to share it — not to blame, but to be honest about how it's affected me. Can you just listen?"*

Use the prompt below to help you or use "I" statements to describe the impact rather than accusations about intent. This keeps the door open for empathy.

## Prompt

"When _____ happened, I felt _____

because _____. What I needed most

in that moment was _____ ."

Then pause. Let your partner respond with something like: *"Thank you for trusting me with that. I can see how that hurt you. I want to understand and help us heal."*

This isn't about fixing — it's about witnessing.

## Share

After the conversation, take a quiet moment together to reflect:

- What did it feel like to speak this truth?

- What did it feel like to simply listen without defending or interrupting?

- What small next step could help repair the hurt — an apology, a check-in, a gesture of care?

Remember: Forgiveness doesn't erase the past, but it creates space for something new to grow in its place.

*Pursuers gather emotion. Withdrawers gather information.*
*Both are seeking safety — just in different ways.*

**RelationTip for the Pursuer:** You may have to let your body settle before reaching out again. That's okay. Give space for calm to return, then approach with softness instead of urgency. Connection can't be forced — it's invited.

**RelationTip for the Withdrawer:** You may have to allow your nervous system to calm, gather your thoughts, and then come back. That's normal. Just make sure to come back to one another and try again.

# Day 58: Empathizing with the Experience

Forgiveness is not a single act — it's a daily decision to loosen your grip on resentment and hold onto love instead. When we choose forgiveness, we aren't saying, "What you did was okay." We're saying, "I refuse to let this pain control me anymore."

But before forgiveness can take root, we have to *understand* what happened — in ourselves and in each other. That's where empathy begins. Empathy invites us to step inside the moment of hurt with curiosity instead of judgment. It asks, *"What was happening in me then? What was happening in you?"*

In the **HEART Model™,** this is the **E — Empathize with the Experience.** It's the gentle work of seeing beyond behavior to the emotion, fear, or unmet need underneath. Empathy doesn't excuse or erase what happened; it simply helps us see the human story beneath the pain. And once we can see, compassion begins to grow where blame once lived.

Forgiveness, then, becomes both a boundary and a bridge. It keeps you anchored in your worth while opening your heart toward repair (Brown, 2012). It's not about forgetting the past; it's about remembering it differently — without letting it define your future (Johnson, 2008).

## Reflect

Think of the hurt you identified yesterday. Step into that moment again — not to relive it, but to see it more clearly.

* What do you think was happening inside of you when it occurred?

* What might have been happening inside your partner?

* What emotions, fears, or unmet needs were present for each of you?

## Engage

With openness and curiosity, talk through what you each remember feeling beneath the surface of that moment. You might say, "I think I felt dismissed, but really I was afraid I didn't matter." Stay curious about your partner's inner world, too — empathy grows when you try to understand, not defend.

## Prompt

"When that moment happened, I think you might have been feeling

_____, and I was feeling _____.

Knowing that helps me see _____."

## Share

Listen to one another's experiences with tenderness. Avoid fixing or correcting. This isn't about agreement — it's about understanding. Simply acknowledge what you hear: "That makes sense. I can see how that felt painful." End with gratitude for each other's honesty — empathy is one of the most sacred forms of repair.

**RelationTip:** Forgiveness grows in understanding. When you can see the hurt through your partner's eyes — and let them see it through yours — compassion begins to replace resentment.

# Day 59: Acknowledge Responsibility

Forgiveness deepens when both partners take responsibility for their part in the hurt — not to assign blame, but to create healing. Acknowledging responsibility says, "I see where I contributed to the pain, and I care enough to make it right."

This step of the **HEART Model™ - A – Acknowledge Responsibility** - invites honesty with humility. Taking ownership doesn't mean carrying all the weight; it means naming your impact with compassion and clarity. Responsibility is the bridge between empathy and repair — it's where understanding turns into action.

Dr. Brené Brown (2018) reminds us that accountability is "a vulnerable process that requires courage, compassion, and connection." When both people can face what went wrong without shame or defensiveness, they open the door to genuine reconciliation.

## Reflect

Think about the situation you've been working with this week.

- What part of this experience do you need to take ownership of?
- Were there words, tones, or reactions that may have added to the hurt?
- What might your partner need to hear acknowledged to feel seen?

## Engage

Take turns sharing what you each want to own about your part in the hurt. Keep it focused on impact, not intent. For example: "I didn't mean to dismiss you, but I see how my reaction made you feel alone." Avoid "yes, but" statements — they undo accountability.

## Prompt

"I take responsibility for _____, and I understand that it made you feel _____. What I wish I had done differently is _____."

## Share

After both of you have shared, take a moment to simply listen and validate each other's efforts. You might say, "Thank you for owning that. It helps me trust that we're moving forward together." If emotions rise, pause and breathe — repair requires patience as much as truth.

**RelationTip:** Accountability isn't about guilt; it's about growth. When you take responsibility for your impact, you're not reliving the past — you're rewriting the future of your relationship.

# Day 60: Releasing the Resentment

Releasing resentment doesn't mean pretending you're fine — it means freeing yourself from carrying what no longer serves your healing. Resentment is heavy; it keeps you tethered to pain and robs you of peace. Letting go isn't about erasing the past, but about reclaiming your energy for what's possible now.

This step of the **HEART Model™ - R – Releasing the Resentment** - is not about quick forgiveness or forced closure. It's a slow unwinding — an invitation to loosen the grip of bitterness one layer at a time. As Dr. Sue Johnson (2008) reminds us, healing comes when we can share our pain and feel met with empathy, not defense. Sometimes release looks like softening toward your partner. Sometimes it looks like softening toward yourself.

Forgiveness is not an arrival; it's a practice of releasing, again and again, until peace begins to take root.

## Reflect

Think about the hurt you've been exploring this week.

- What are you still holding onto — anger, sadness, fear, disappointment?
- How has carrying this resentment affected your heart, body, or connection?
- What might you make space for if you began to let it go?

## Engage

Gently write a few sentences describing what you're ready to release — even if it's just one small piece of the pain. You might say, "I'm ready to let go of the story that I have to protect myself all the time," or "I'm ready to release the expectation that they'll make it right in a specific way."

If this feels too soon, honor that. Readiness for release is a form of wisdom, not weakness.

_____

_____

_____

## Prompt

"Today, I choose to begin releasing _____ because holding onto it keeps me from _____."

## Share

If it feels safe, share your reflection with your partner. You might say, "I'm not finished forgiving, but I want you to know I'm trying to make space for peace."
The listener's only job is to hold space — no defending, no fixing. Just presence. End by expressing gratitude for the courage it takes to do this work.

**RelationTip:** Release doesn't mean forget; it means you've decided your peace matters more than your pain. Every time you let go, even a little, you lighten the load — and make more room for love to grow.

# Day 61: Turn Toward Repair

Repair is where healing takes root. It's not about erasing what happened — it's about choosing to reach for one another again, with honesty, humility, and hope. This step of the **HEART Model™ — T – Turn Toward Repair** — is where insight becomes action and compassion becomes connection.

Dr. John Gottman (1999) found that repair attempts — those small moments when one partner reaches out to reconnect — are the single greatest predictors of lasting love. Repair doesn't demand perfection; it just requires effort. Every "I'm sorry," every gentle touch, every "Can we start again?" becomes a thread that reweaves trust.

Repairing doesn't mean the pain disappears. It means you're building a bridge strong enough to hold it — together.

## Reflect

Think about what repair would look like in your current situation.

- What would help your relationship feel reconnected?
- What do you most need from your partner as you move forward?
- What are you willing to offer to rebuild safety and trust?

## Engage

Talk with your partner about one small, tangible way you can turn toward each other this week. It might be scheduling a check-in, planning a gentle conversation, or sharing a moment of appreciation. Keep it simple — repair thrives in small, consistent gestures.

## Prompt

"One way I want to turn toward you this week is _____
_____ because I want us to _____
_____."

## Share

When you share, focus on hope and collaboration rather than blame or history. Listen with open hearts and soft eyes. End by affirming your shared commitment to growth: "I know we can do this together."

Then, express gratitude for the courage it took to engage this process — forgiveness is never easy, but it's always worth it.

**RelationTip:** Repair isn't the end of the story — it's the beginning of a new one. When two people turn toward each other after pain, they prove that love isn't fragile. It's resilient.

# Day 62: The Grace of Letting Go

*"Not forgiving is like drinking rat poison and then waiting for the rat to die."*
**— Anne Lamott (1997)**

There comes a moment in every healing journey when holding on hurts more than letting go.
Resentment feels like protection — but it's really exhaustion. It keeps us tethered to pain that no longer serves who we're becoming.

Forgiveness asks us to loosen our grip — not on truth, but on bitterness. It doesn't excuse the hurt or erase accountability. It simply says, *"I'm ready to stop carrying what's been breaking my back."*

Research continues to affirm what love already knows: letting go heals. Chronic anger and resentment keep the body in a state of alert, raising cortisol and blood pressure, while forgiveness has been linked to lower stress, improved mood, and even better heart health (The Forgiveness Project, n.d.).

When we let go, we're not denying the wound — we're choosing not to live from it anymore.

## Reflect

What pain or resentment still lingers in you — toward your partner or yourself?
What has it cost you to hold on?
What might begin to heal if you started to let go?

## Engage

This isn't about a single moment of release — it's about practice. Write down the story, emotion, or memory that feels ready to soften.

Then, say quietly:
"I release what no longer serves my heart. I choose peace, even if I have to choose it again tomorrow."

## Prompt

"I've been carrying _____,

and it has made me feel _____.

Today, I choose to begin letting it go so I can make space for _____

_____."

## Share

If it feels right, tell your partner what you're releasing — not for reassurance, but as a declaration of freedom.
Let silence follow. Sometimes, healing doesn't need words; it needs breath.

**RelationTip:** Letting go isn't weakness — it's wisdom. It's the sacred act of saying, "This pain shaped me, but it doesn't define me."

# Day 63: The Courage to Begin Again

Forgiveness doesn't erase the past — it redeems it.
It gives new meaning to what once felt unbearable and allows love to breathe again in the places that were gasping for air.

This week, you've practiced the courage to face what hurts, the grace to let go, and the humility to reach for repair. You've lived the rhythm of the HEART Model™ — even if you didn't realize it — turning wounds into windows of deeper understanding.

To begin again isn't to start from scratch; it's to stand on the ground of what you've learned and build forward, stronger, softer, wiser.

Dr. Sue Johnson (2008) reminds us that healing happens not in grand gestures, but in the small, daily choices to reach back across the distance — to touch a hand, meet a gaze, and whisper, *"I'm still here."*

## Reflect

What shifted in you this week?
Where do you feel even a little more free, soft, or open?
What do you want to carry with you as you move forward?

## Engage

Write a brief statement of gratitude or commitment to your partner — something that honors the work you've done together.
Example:
"Thank you for staying in the process with me. I want to keep choosing grace, even when it's hard."

Read your words to each other — slowly, with eye contact.

## Prompt

"I want to begin again with _____.
I'm grateful for _____, and I'm
hopeful about _____."

## Share

Close this week however feels true to you — a hug, a walk, prayer, silence, or laughter. You don't need to be finished to begin again. You just need to stay willing.

**RelationTip:** Every love story worth living will require repair. Beginning again isn't the end of the story — it's the proof that your love still has a heartbeat.

# WEEK 10

# THE WORK OF TRUST

# Week 10: The Work of Trust

Trust is the quiet heartbeat of a healthy relationship. It's what allows us to exhale, to soften, and to lean in when life gets hard. When trust is strong, love feels safe — not just exciting. When it's fragile, everything else begins to tremble.

But trust isn't only about fidelity. It's about emotional reliability — being honest, consistent, and safe. It's about knowing that when you reach out, your partner will be there. That your story will be held with care. That even when there's rupture, repair will follow (Gottman, 2015).

Like many other relational muscles, trust is built in the quiet moments that often go unnoticed — the check-in text that says, *"I'm thinking about you."* The apology that comes without defensiveness. The conversation where curiosity replaces criticism. The follow-through on what you promised. These small moments are what shape security over time.

This week, you'll reflect on where trust feels strong and where it still feels tender. You'll explore what trust really means to each of you — and what it takes to nurture or rebuild it.

Building trust requires courage. The courage to tell the truth, even when it's uncomfortable. The courage to show up authentically and admit when you're wrong. The courage to stay kind and curious, especially when fear or defensiveness wants to take over.

Trust isn't static — it evolves. It deepens with time, with presence, and with practice. If it's been broken, it can be rebuilt. But that rebuilding doesn't happen through time alone; it happens through transparency, consistency, and care. It's a process of showing up, again and again, with honesty and heart.

Whether you're strengthening trust, repairing it, or simply learning to rest in it, this week is about moving closer — to each other, and to the kind of love that can hold your full story.

"Trust is the glue of life. It's the foundational principle that holds all relationships." — Stephen Covey (1989)

Let's begin the work — gently, together.

# Day 64: What Does Trust Mean to You?

Trust is one of those words we all use but rarely stop to define. We talk about it like it's universal — until a moment of disappointment reminds us that what "trust" means to one person may not mean the same to another.

For one partner, trust might mean emotional honesty — being willing to say what's true, even when it's hard. For another, it might mean dependability — the confidence that promises will be kept. And for others, trust may look like emotional safety, consistency, or being able to share openly without fear of judgment (Gottman, 2015).

When we don't define trust, we end up chasing it — assuming it looks like the version we learned from our past. Today is about pausing to name what trust really means to you — and to listen carefully to what it means to your partner — so you can build it with clarity and care.

## Reflect

What does trust mean to you?

- What does it feel like in your body when you trust your partner?
- How do you know when it's present — or when it's missing?
- What moments have built (or repaired) trust between you so far?

## Engage

Write out your definitions of trust: _____

_____

_____

## Prompt

Complete the statement that feels truest for you: "To me, trust looks like _____ because _____

_____."or simply, "To me, trust is _____

_____."

## Share

After sharing, talk about what surprised you or stood out. Did you learn anything new about how your partner experiences trust? Discuss one way you can honor their definition moving forward.

End by affirming one another: "I want to keep earning your trust — not just by what I say, but by how I show up."

**RelationTip:** We often say, "If you would just trust me…" — but trust can't be demanded. It's not a switch to flip; it's a rhythm you build. Trust = Time + Consistency (Chafee, 2003).

# Day 65: Sharing Moments of Trust

Trust isn't built in a promise — it's built in a pattern.
It grows through a collection of remembered moments: when words align with actions, when care follows conflict, when presence replaces pretense. Over time, these moments weave together to create something sacred — a steady sense that *I can lean on you, and you'll still be there.*

Trust forms in the spaces where safety is practiced, not just promised. It's the late-night conversation that ends in reassurance instead of retreat. It's the moment your partner says, "I'll handle it," and actually does. It's the willingness to come back after misunderstanding — not perfectly, but honestly.

Each act of consistency, accountability, or tenderness becomes a brick in the foundation of safety. When enough of those bricks stack up, the heart begins to rest.

If you've ever navigated hard seasons together, you already know that trust isn't a feeling that appears overnight — it's a confidence that grows from experience. And even when it's been fractured, trust can be rebuilt through transparency, empathy, and follow-through.

Today's practice is an opportunity to pause and recognize where that trust has already taken root — not as perfection, but as progress.

## Reflect

Think about the small, specific ways your partner has built or rebuilt trust with you.

## Engage

Write those moments out below. Be as concrete as possible — describe what happened, what you felt, and what it meant to you. These are the threads that quietly weave safety into your story.

_____

_____

_____

## Prompt

"I trusted you when _____ and I felt reassured because _____."

## Share

Talk about how those moments shaped your relationship. How did trust grow through those experiences? How does it feel to hear your partner recall a moment when you earned their trust?

Let yourself take it in. You've both worked to create this foundation — and it deserves to be seen.

**RelationTip:** When your partner names a moment they trusted you, don't rush past it. Let it land. Let it matter. That's where connection deepens — in the recognition of what's already been healed.

# Day 66: Rebuilding Trust

Every relationship faces moments when trust wobbles. Sometimes it's a small misunderstanding; other times, it's a deeper wound that shakes your sense of safety. When that happens, you stand at a cross-roads: retreat into protection or move toward repair with honesty, consistency, and care.

Trust isn't rebuilt in dramatic declarations or one-time apologies. It's rebuilt in the quiet, repeated follow-through — when words begin to match actions, when effort replaces avoidance, and when reliability starts to feel steady again (Gottman, 2015).

These small but consistent moments of truth-telling and accountability become the scaffolding for safety. Over time, the nervous system begins to relax, the heart begins to believe, and the relationship begins to breathe again.

Today's work invites you to look at those places where trust still feels tender — not to reopen wounds, but to name what needs healing and to take one step closer to restoring safety and connection (Johnson, 2008).

## Reflect

Think of a time when trust was tested or strained.

- What happened, and how did it affect your sense of closeness?
- What emotions surface when you recall it — hurt, fear, disappointment, shame?
- What would healing look like if you both leaned in?

## Engage

Together, name one area where trust could be strengthened.
Use "I" statements to express your needs clearly, without blame.
For example: *"I felt anxious when you didn't follow through,"* or
*"I need consistency to feel secure again."*

## Prompt

"I felt uncertain when _____

_____ and I think we can strengthen our trust by _____

_____."

## Share

As your partner shares, listen with openness and empathy. Try not
to defend or explain — just receive. Ask, *"What would help you feel
safer with me again?"* and then follow through.

This is the work — not perfection, but presence.

**RelationTip:** Rebuilding trust isn't about earning a flawless record.
It's about showing, over time, that love can hold what broke. Repair
happens one consistent, compassionate choice at a time.

# Day 67: Practicing Openness and Accountability

Trust thrives where truth feels safe.

It's not built through perfection, but through the daily practice of honesty — staying open when it would be easier to close off, and taking responsibility when we fall short. Openness and accountability are twin muscles that grow stronger each time we choose curiosity over defense and ownership over blame (Brown, 2012).

Amber and I learned this during a parenting moment that could have easily divided us. Our teenage son had broken a boundary around social media, and emotions were running high. I wanted to address it immediately — to fix the problem before it spiraled. Amber wanted to wait — to give him time to reflect before we talked. My urgency felt to her like pressure; her calm felt to me like avoidance. Underneath it all, we were both just trying to protect what mattered most: trust.

Later that night, we talked it through. I shared that my need to "solve it now" came from fear — a fear of losing control. She shared that her pause came from compassion — she didn't want shame to close him off. Once we both owned what was happening inside of us, the tension began to dissolve.

That moment reminded me: openness isn't just about being honest *with* your partner — it's also about being honest *about yourself.* It's saying, *"Here's what I'm feeling, and here's what's behind it."* Personal accountability is taking responsibility for your emotions instead of making your partner responsible for managing them.

When openness meets accountability, truth feels safe again. You can tell the truth without fear. You can own your reactions without shame. And trust begins to rebuild, one grounded moment at a time.

## Reflect

Think about a recent moment of tension.

- Were you open about what was happening inside you, or did you expect your partner to read your emotions?
- How might taking responsibility for your feelings shift the tone of those conversations?

## Engage

Share one way you want to practice greater openness and one way you want to take more ownership for your emotional responses this week. Use the prompt below if you need help.

## Prompt

"I can be more open with you by _____,

and I can be more accountable for my emotions by _____

_____."

## Share

Take turns talking about what makes it safe to be honest — and what makes it hard. End by affirming that openness isn't weakness and accountability isn't blame. They're both forms of love in motion.

**RelationTip:**
Being open means inviting your partner into your truth. Being accountable means standing steady in it. When you practice both, honesty becomes a bridge instead of a battlefield.

# Day 68: The Weight of Broken Promises

Even the strongest relationships have moments when trust takes a hit. Sometimes it's something small — forgetting a commitment or not following through on a promise. Other times, it's bigger — a repeated pattern that quietly erodes safety. Broken promises, no matter their size, leave an emotional imprint because they touch the most tender part of love: the belief that we can depend on one another (Johnson, 2008).

When a promise is broken, it's not just the action that hurts — it's what the action communicates: *"You weren't there when I needed you."* That wound can stir feelings of disappointment, fear, and even shame. But the good news is this: every broken promise also carries an invitation — to acknowledge, to repair, and to rebuild something stronger than before (Gottman, 2015).

Rebuilding doesn't start with defensiveness or explanations; it begins with empathy and ownership. When we own our missteps, we offer our partner a bridge back to safety — not by perfection, but by presence.

## Reflect

Think about a time when a promise was broken — either by you or your partner.

## Engage

Write down that moment.

_____

_____

_____

## Prompt

"One promise that felt broken was _____

_____. What would help me heal is _____

_____."

## Share

Take turns reflecting on how you both respond when trust falters. Discuss what accountability, follow-through, and reassurance could look like moving forward. The goal isn't to rehash pain — it's to create a shared plan for repair.

**RelationTip:** Broken promises can feel heavy, but healing begins the moment we choose truth over pride. When we own what hurt, we give love the chance to breathe again — and that's where trust begins to regrow.

# Day 69: The Power of Follow-Through

Trust grows in the soil of consistency.

Every time you do what you say you'll do — even in the smallest way — your relationship becomes just a little safer. Promises kept over time build the steady rhythm of dependability that allows both partners to relax and lean in (Gottman, 2015).

Follow-through isn't about perfection; it's about intention. It's the quiet *"I've got you"* moments — the text you actually send, the errand you follow through on, the apology you don't delay. Those choices may seem small, but they communicate something profound: *You can count on me.*

When we repeatedly fail to follow through, even unintentionally, it creates micro-fractures in the bond. Over time, those tiny cracks can widen into emotional distance. Repair begins when we make our reliability visible through the daily rhythm of keeping our word (Johnson, 2008).

## Reflect

Think about a time your partner followed through in a way that really mattered to you — maybe something simple but deeply reassuring.

- What message did that action send to your nervous system?
- How did it impact your sense of safety or connection?

## Engage

Together, name one small, consistent action each of you can take this week to show reliability. Keep it doable — something that builds momentum and trust over time. Use the prompt if you need help.

## Prompt

"One way I can practice better follow-through is _____

_____, because it will help my partner feel

_____."

## Share

Take a few moments to talk about how it feels when your partner follows through.

What emotions or sensations arise in your body when they keep their word? Relief? Ease? Gratitude? Then, share how it feels on the other side — when *you* follow through.

Notice how reliability creates calm for both of you, even in small ways.

**RelationTip:** Follow-through is love in motion. It tells your partner, *I see you, I hear you, and I mean what I say.* Trust isn't rebuilt by words — it's rebuilt by walking them out, one promise at a time.

# Day 70: Reassurance and Repair

As we close this week on trust, remember this: safety in a relationship isn't built by avoiding rupture — it's built by learning how to return after it. Every couple drifts, misses, and misunderstands. But secure relationships don't fall apart because of disconnection; they heal through repair (Johnson, 2008).

Repair always begins with reassurance.

It's the small, steady gestures that whisper, *"We're still us."* The glance across the room after tension. The text that says, *"I didn't mean to hurt you."* The gentle hand that reaches out first. Reassurance tells the nervous system, *"You're safe again."* It helps both partners step out of defense and back into connection.

Repair grows out of that reassurance.

It's the active choice to name what happened, take ownership, and rebuild trust through care and consistency. Repair isn't about erasing pain; it's about tending to it. It's saying, *"Our bond matters more than being right."*
Each time we reach back after hurt, we teach each other that safety can survive the storm.

As this week comes to a close, take a breath and notice how far you've come. Trust isn't a finish line — it's a rhythm of reassurance and repair, practiced again and again until it becomes part of the heartbeat of your relationship.

## Reflect

Think about a recent moment of tension or hurt.

- What helped you both find your way back?
- Did you or your partner offer reassurance?

- What did that gesture communicate?

## Engage

Share one small way you've practiced reassurance or repair this week. Notice how it changed the atmosphere between you. What helped you soften? What helped you stay open?

## Prompt

"When we repair after conflict, what helps me feel most reassured is _____, because it reminds me _____."

## Share

Take a few minutes to talk about how you both want to continue this rhythm in the weeks ahead.
What does reassurance sound like for each of you? What kind of repair feels most healing?
End by affirming the work you've done this week — the honesty, the follow-through, the courage to keep showing up.

### RelationTip:
Reassurance and repair are the quiet superpowers of trust. They remind us that love doesn't need perfection — it just needs two people willing to reach back for each other, again and again.

# WEEK 11

# HOLDING THE GOOD

# Week 11: Holding the Good

Last week, you did some hard emotional work — the kind that deepens trust, not just between you and your partner, but within yourself. If you made it through those conversations with honesty and care, take a moment to feel proud. That's no small thing. Now it's time to shift toward something equally powerful — holding the good.

> *"Gratitude is the most exquisite form of courtesy."*
> — **Jacques Maritain**

Gratitude is more than good manners; it's a mindset, a posture of the heart that recognizes what's working instead of only what's broken. It's saying, *I see what's right about us, even when life feels messy.* When we practice gratitude, we're not ignoring what needs repair — we're balancing the story. We're reminding our hearts that there is beauty here, too.

Research consistently shows that gratitude is one of the most powerful predictors of long-term relational health. When couples make a habit of noticing and naming what they appreciate in each other, they report greater satisfaction, stronger communication, and deeper emotional connection (Algoe, 2012; Gordon et al., 2012; Emmons & McCullough, 2003). In fact, gratitude has been shown to activate the same neural pathways that increase empathy and reduce conflict — literally wiring our brains for connection (Fox et al., 2015).

In emotionally secure relationships, gratitude becomes a form of emotional regulation. When tension rises, a simple moment of appreciation — a thank-you, a touch, a kind word — can bring both partners back to center. It reminds us that love isn't built by keeping score; it's built by seeing the good, again and again.

This week is about practicing that art — slowing down long enough to notice what's beautiful, kind, or steady in your relationship and letting your partner know it matters. You'll reflect, name, and express appreciation in ways that feel authentic to you. You don't have to force positivity. You just have to stay open to noticing what's already good — and then say it out loud.

Let's begin.

# Day 71: Simply Noticing

*"Gratitude turns what we have into enough."*
**— Aesop**

It's easy to notice what's missing. The undone chores, the unspoken words, the missed moments — our brains are wired to scan for problems before positives. But relationships flourish when we learn to slow that reflex and intentionally look for what's good.

Noticing the good doesn't mean pretending everything's perfect. It means widening your lens — choosing to see the effort, the care, the quiet gestures that say, *I'm still here.* When we make a habit of gratitude, we change not only how we see our partner, but how our nervous system feels around them. Safety grows where appreciation lives (Algoe, 2012; Gordon et al., 2012).

Today is about retraining your awareness. You don't have to manufacture grand gratitude — just start noticing the small, ordinary things your partner does that make life a little lighter.

## Reflect

Take a few moments to think about what your partner has done recently — this week, or even today — that made you feel seen, supported, or valued.

It might be something as simple as a kind word, a small task done without being asked, or a moment of tenderness when you needed it most.

## Engage

Write down three specific things your partner did (or often does) that you appreciate.

1. _____

2. _____

3. ._____

## Prompt

"Something you did recently that meant a lot to me was _____.
It made me feel _____ because
_____."

## Share

Take a moment to share your list with your partner — or leave it somewhere for them to find. Notice how your body feels when you express appreciation out loud. Gratitude softens defenses and strengthens connection (Emmons & McCullough, 2003).

**RelationTip:** The more you notice the good, the easier it becomes to find it. Gratitude is like muscle memory — the more you practice, the more natural it feels.

# Day 72: Speaking Appreciation Out Loud

*"Feeling gratitude and not expressing it is like wrapping a present and not giving it."*
— **William Arthur Ward**

Noticing what we're grateful for is powerful — but speaking it aloud is what transforms a good thought into connection. When appreciation stays silent, it loses impact. But when it's voiced, it nourishes both people — the giver and the receiver.

Verbal gratitude creates a feedback loop of safety. It tells your partner, *I see you. You matter. You make a difference.* It shifts the emotional climate of your relationship from one of assumption to one of affirmation. Expressing gratitude aloud has been shown to increase oxytocin and emotional closeness in couples, fostering mutual safety and satisfaction (Algoe, Fredrickson, & Gable, 2013; Gordon et al., 2012).

Today's focus is to put words to the good you've already noticed — to turn gratitude into expression.

## Reflect

Think about how you usually express appreciation.

- Do you say "thank you" often, or do you assume your partner already knows how you feel?

- What makes it easy or difficult for you to verbalize gratitude?

- How does your partner tend to show appreciation — through words, actions, or presence?

## Engage

Choose one specific thing your partner has done recently that you truly appreciated.

Then, tell them — out loud. Be direct, sincere, and specific. Use the prompt below to guide your conversation.

## Prompt

"When you _____, it meant a lot to me because _____. I felt _____, and I want to thank you for that."

## Share

After sharing, notice your partner's response — not just in words, but in posture, eye contact, or warmth. Ask them what kind of appreciation feels most meaningful to them.

**RelationTip:** Appreciation builds emotional safety like deposits in a bank. The more you express it, the stronger the foundation becomes — especially when life gets hard.

# Day 73: Gratitude in Everyday Moments

*"Enjoy the little things, for one day you may look back and realize they were the big things."*
**— Robert Brault**

Gratitude doesn't have to wait for milestones, anniversaries, or special moments.
In fact, the healthiest relationships are built on daily appreciation — the kind that shows up in passing smiles, quiet gestures, and the small, steady moments that often go unnoticed.

When we slow down enough to see those ordinary moments for what they are — evidence of love in motion — we begin to shift the emotional current of the relationship. Gratitude becomes less about grand statements and more about quiet awareness.

Today is about finding the sacred in the simple.

## Reflect

Think about your ordinary days — mornings, commutes, chores, meals, evenings. Where do you see your partner's love showing up in subtle ways? Maybe it's how they pour your coffee, check in with a text, or keep the house peaceful after a long day.

# Engage

Write down a few examples of how love hides in your everyday routines:

1. _____

2. _____

3. ._____


# Prompt

Complete this sentence: "One small thing you do that I often overlook, but deeply appreciate, is _____. It reminds me that our love lives in the ordinary."

# Share

Tell your partner how you felt *hearing* their gratitude.

**RelationTip:** Gratitude isn't built in big moments; it's built in the ordinary ones we choose to notice. The more you look for goodness, the more goodness you'll find.

# Day 74: Showing Gratitude Through Action

*"Love is something you do for someone else,*
*not something you feel."*
**— Gary Chapman**

Gratitude is powerful when spoken — but transformational when practiced.

When we turn appreciation into action, we create an emotional echo that lingers far beyond words. It tells your partner, *I don't just love you — I see you, I value you, and I want to make your life lighter.*

Behavioral expressions of gratitude — like small gestures or acts of service — have been shown to increase relationship satisfaction and reinforce secure attachment by signaling emotional investment and attunement (Algoe, 2012; Gordon et al., 2012; Lambert & Fincham, 2011).

These gestures don't have to be elaborate. They can be as simple as a note tucked in a bag, doing a task your partner normally handles, or offering undivided attention during a stressful day. Gratitude through action says: *I remember what matters to you — and I care enough to act on it.*

## Reflect

Think of one way your partner has shown up for you recently — something they did that made your day easier, brighter, or calmer. How did it make you feel?

Now, shift your focus inward. Where could you mirror that same kind of care? What's one small action that would let your partner feel seen and appreciated — not just through words, but through presence and follow-through?

## Engage

Choose one simple, tangible way to express gratitude today. It might mean finishing a task before they ask, sending a note of encouragement, or carving out space for them to rest.

Whatever you do, let it say, *I see what matters to you — and I'm choosing to nurture it.*

## Prompt

"An action I can take today to show my gratitude is _____ _____ because I know it will make you feel _____."

## Share

After you've carried out your gesture, take a quiet moment together. Notice how it felt to *give* or *receive* gratitude through action.

Ask, "What gestures make you feel most appreciated?" and listen with curiosity. These small insights become the building blocks of emotional connection.

**RelationTip:** Gratitude in words fills the heart. Gratitude in action fills the space between you. When love is both spoken and lived, safety and joy naturally follow.

# Day 75: Gratitude for the Storms

Every relationship weathers storms — the kind that test our patience, faith, and love. But when you make it through, something shifts. Beneath the scar tissue, there's often something sacred: a deeper sense of gratitude, resilience, and quiet knowing that *we made it.*

Today's practice is about honoring those storms. Not to relive the pain, but to remember the strength that got you through — and the love that kept you tethered when everything else was shaking.

Gratitude after adversity has been shown to strengthen emotional regulation, deepen connection, and reduce physiological stress responses by helping couples make meaning out of hardship (Fredrickson, 2004; Porges, 2011; van der Kolk, 2014).

## Reflect

Think of a difficult season you've faced together — a loss, a rupture, or a moment of uncertainty.

* What did you endure as a couple?
* How did this challenge shape your understanding of love or safety?

Now, tune in to your body. Notice what happens as you remember that season.
Does your chest soften?
Do your eyes well up?
Do you feel warmth, tension, pride, or relief?
Whatever you notice — let it be there. That's your body saying, *this mattered.*

## Engage

Take turns sharing your memory using this simple, grounding phrase: "I remember when we went through _____. The way we navigated that together made me feel _____. Thank you for showing up for us — and for me." Speak slowly. Let the words find their weight.

## Prompt

After sharing, pause for a few moments of silence.

Then say: "When I remember that time, my body feels _____ _____ because _____."
Let the focus stay on what's alive in the present — the gratitude that lingers after the storm.

## Share

End with a moment of shared stillness. Maybe it's holding hands, sharing a quiet smile, or simply sitting together without words. Allow the memory — and the meaning — to settle between you.

**RelationTip:** Our bodies store what our minds can't always name. Gratitude helps release what's been held too long, turning old pain into present peace. When you honor the storms you've survived, you remind each other that love is not fragile — it's forged.

# Day 76: Gratitude as a Daily Practice

*"Gratitude turns ordinary days into thanksgiving, routine jobs into joy, and ordinary opportunities into blessings."*
— **William Arthur Ward**

Gratitude is not a destination — it's a discipline. The real transformation happens when appreciation becomes the rhythm of your daily life. In relationships, consistent gratitude builds emotional security. It reminds your partner that their presence matters, their effort is noticed, and their love leaves an imprint.

This practice doesn't have to be elaborate — it just has to be consistent. The small act of saying "thank you" or noticing the good is what rewires the relationship from reactive to receptive. Regular gratitude practice has been shown to strengthen neural pathways for empathy, optimism, and relational satisfaction (Emmons & McCullough, 2003; Fox et al., 2015).

## Reflect

Think about what helps you stay mindful of the good in your relationship.

Is it slowing down before bed to name what went right? Writing a note? Pausing in the middle of a busy day to notice the way your partner makes life easier?

## Engage

Commit to a daily gratitude ritual this week — something small but specific.

It could be:

- Saying one thing you appreciate about your partner before sleep.
- Sending a text during the day to acknowledge something kind.
- Keeping a shared gratitude journal.

## Prompt

"One way I will practice gratitude daily is _____

_____ because it will help me remember

_____."

## Share

End the day by telling your partner one thing you noticed or appreciated today. This habit, repeated over time, becomes the heartbeat of connection.

**RelationTip:** Gratitude isn't something you feel your way into — it's something you practice your way into. When gratitude becomes a rhythm, love becomes a reflex.

# Day 77: Reflecting on Holding the Good

Gratitude is one of the most sustaining forces in love — not because it ignores what's hard, but because it helps us remember what's still worth fighting for. This week, you've practiced noticing, naming, and living out appreciation. You've looked back at the storms, found beauty in the ordinary, and discovered how gratitude transforms both heart and home. Today is about reflecting on how those practices have shifted you — even subtly.

Daily gratitude practices have been shown to strengthen emotional resilience, regulate stress, and increase long-term relational satisfaction by reinforcing positive emotional memory (Emmons & Mc-Cullough, 2003; Algoe, 2012; Fredrickson, 2004).

## Reflect

How has gratitude changed the way you see your partner?
Your relationship?
Yourself?
What feels lighter, stronger, or more grounded as a result?

## Engage

Write down your biggest take away from this weeks' work.

_____

_____

_____

## Prompt

"Something I want to keep practicing from this week is _____
_____ because
_____."

## Share

Close the week with a gesture of appreciation — a note, a touch, a simple "thank you." Let this be your full-circle moment: gratitude not just spoken, but embodied.

**RelationTip:** Gratitude keeps love awake. The more you practice noticing the good, the more good there is to notice.

# WEEK 12

# FILLING YOUR OWN CUP

# Week 12: Filling Your Own Cup

Self-care isn't selfish — it's sacred.

It's an act of relational integrity, a quiet promise to tend to your own heart so that you can show up fully for the ones you love.

In relationships, neglecting self-care doesn't just wear us down; it wears down the bond itself. It leads to burnout, resentment, and emotional disconnection. But when we take responsibility for our emotional, mental, physical, and spiritual well-being, something powerful happens — we become more grounded, compassionate, and available. We stop giving from depletion and begin giving from overflow.

Research shows that self-care practices and emotional regulation directly improve relationship satisfaction, reduce stress hormones, and increase empathy and co-regulation between partners (Neff, 2011; Porges, 2011; Reis et al., 2018).

Think of self-care as both a boundary and a bridge. It sets limits that protect your energy and also creates pathways for deeper intimacy and respect. It says, "I matter, and so do you." In that space, love grows from shared wholeness rather than constant sacrifice.

This week, we'll reframe self-care as a shared investment in the life you're building together. You'll explore what fills you up, what drains you, and how to communicate those truths with honesty and grace. You'll practice rest, reflection, play, and boundaries — not as luxuries, but as lifelines. Because when you nurture your inner world, your outer relationship begins to bloom.

You'll also learn to support each other's self-care without taking it personally — to hold space when your partner needs solitude, to cheer them on when they're pursuing what brings them alive, and to trust that distance doesn't mean disconnection. It means you're both doing the work of staying whole.

By the end of this week, we hope you'll see self-care not as one more thing to fit in, but as the foundation that holds everything else together. It's the ongoing practice of returning to yourself so you can return to one another with love that's steady, generous, and real.

Take a breath. You've poured a lot into this journey so far.

Now, it's time to refill.

# Day 78: The Importance of Self-Care in Your Relationship

*"To love someone well is to give them space to breathe and grow, while also staying close enough to offer support and connection when needed."*
**— Dr. John Gottman**

We often think of self-care as something we do alone — a solo walk, a quiet morning, a moment to reset. But in truth, self-care is one of the most relational things we can practice. When you care for yourself, you're tending to the part of you that shows up in your relationship. You're saying to your partner, "I want to bring you the best of me, not what's left of me."

Healthy relationships are built between two people who know how to return to center — who can recognize when they're running on empty and take responsibility for refilling. When both partners practice self-care, they create a rhythm of balance: time together that feels alive and time apart that restores it.

## Reflect

What role does self-care currently play in your relationship? How does tending to your individual well-being contribute to the health of your connection as a couple?

## Engage

Talk together about the ways you each practice self-care — physically, emotionally, spiritually, and mentally. Are there ways you could better support each other in those practices?

## Prompt

"Taking care of myself is important for our relationship because __

_____

_____."

## Share

Open up about what self-care looks like for you personally and listen to your partner share the same. Are there new ways you could intentionally protect space for each other's care?

**RelationTip:** Caring for yourself isn't pulling away — it's preparing to come back well. When you value your own self-care, you give your partner permission to rest, too. Love breathes best when both people have space to exhale.

# Day 79: Locating What Fills You

*"When we self-care, we also relationship-care.*
*The more whole we are individually,*
*the more we can show up for each other."*
**— Esther Perel**

So often, we push past what we need — telling ourselves we'll rest later, breathe later, slow down later. But the truth is, when we continually ignore our needs, we end up running on fumes and showing up half-present for the people we love most.

Self-care is not indulgence; it's maintenance for your heart. It's how you refill what life, parenting, work, and relationship naturally pour out. And it's different for everyone — what restores one person may drain another. The goal isn't to copy someone else's rhythm, but to discover your own.

Research consistently shows that regular self-care and emotional attunement increase emotional regulation and satisfaction within intimate relationships (Neff, 2011; Reis et al., 2018).

## Reflect

What do you need today — mentally, emotionally, spiritually, or physically — to feel grounded and well? Have you been ignoring or pushing past that need? When was the last time you felt full — calm, steady, and clear — and what contributed to that?

## Engage

Write down one tangible way you can meet that need today. Is it rest? Movement? Quiet? Time outdoors? Saying no to something that drains you?

_____

_____

_____

## Prompt

"What I need to focus on today for self-care and self-compassion is _____. This will benefit our relationship by _____."

## Share

Tell your partner what today's self-care looks like for you and invite them to reflect on their own.

Consider checking in later to encourage and support each other — reminding each other that rest is not weakness; it's preparation for connection.

**RelationTip:** Self-care is a gift to your relationship. When you care for yourself with intention, you show up with more presence, clarity, and capacity for love.

# Day 80: Holding Space for Yourself

*"Almost everything will work again if you unplug it for a few minutes, including you."*
— **Anne Lamott**

Yesterday, you named what fills you. Today is about protecting it. It's one thing to know what restores you — it's another to guard that space when life gets loud. Between work, family, and the endless pull of responsibility, our most important practices of rest and renewal often become the first things we sacrifice. But restoration isn't a luxury. It's a boundary that says, *"My well-being matters — and so does yours."*

Holding space for yourself doesn't mean withdrawing from your partner; it means staying connected to your own center so you can return to them grounded and present. It's about building rhythms that keep you balanced, kind, and emotionally available. When both partners learn to guard their internal worlds with care, the relationship becomes more peaceful, sustainable, and emotionally safe.

Research shows that couples who prioritize personal restoration report higher relational satisfaction, better conflict recovery, and more emotional regulation (Porges, 2011; Reis et al., 2018).

## Reflect

Think about one practice that truly restores you — the thing that helps you reset when life feels heavy.

## Engage

Write what restores you here: _____

_____

_____

_____

## Prompt

Complete the following reflection together: "When I choose to protect my restoration time by _____

_____, I notice that I feel _____

_____. When I care for myself in this way, I'm able to show up in our relationship with more _____

_____."

## Share

Talk together about how to support each other's restorative rhythms. Ask: *"What helps you feel restored — and how can I help you protect that time?"* Then make a plan together to defend those spaces as a team, not as individuals in competition.

**RelationTip:** Protecting what restores you is not selfish; it's stewardship. You can't offer what you don't have. When both partners guard their energy, love has room to stay generous, patient, and kind.

# Day 81: Honoring Your Partners Space

*"Love is not about merging—it's about witnessing each other's becoming."*
**— Esther Perel**

Yesterday, you focused on protecting your own restoration. Today is about honoring your partner's.

One of the greatest gifts you can give your partner is the freedom to recharge in their own way. Supporting their restoration isn't about fixing, scheduling, or managing their self-care — it's about respecting what helps them feel whole, even when it doesn't include you.

When we're not mindful, it's easy to misinterpret our partner's need for space as rejection. But often, it's not distance they're seeking — it's renewal. The more you can support that, the safer and more connected your relationship becomes.

This practice transforms self-care from an individual act into a shared rhythm. When you both learn to celebrate each other's restoration, you're really saying, *"I want you to be well — because when you thrive, we thrive."*

Research in relationship science confirms that supporting a partner's autonomy and self-expansion fosters security and long-term satisfaction (Deci & Ryan, 2000; Perel, 2006). When both partners feel free to recharge, emotional intimacy deepens naturally.

## Reflect

Think about how your partner restores themselves when life feels heavy. Ask yourself:

- Do I make room for that, or do I resist it?

- How do I typically respond when my partner needs space, rest, or solitude?

- What might it look like to support their restoration without taking it personally?

## Engage

Ask your partner directly: "What helps you feel restored — physically, emotionally, or spiritually — and how can I support that without intruding?" Listen carefully. Your job is not to solve, plan, or critique — just to understand what matters most to them.

## Prompt

Complete this reflection: "One way I can support your restoration is by _____. When I do this, I hope you feel _____."

## Share

Talk about what true support looks like for both of you. Do you need quiet encouragement, practical help, or simply permission to step away without guilt?

**RelationTip:** Supporting your partner's restoration is one of the purest forms of love. It says, *"I trust you to care for yourself — and I'll be here when you come home to you."*

# Day 82: Boundaries Around Self-Care

*"Boundaries are not a wall to keep others out,*
*but a bridge to help both partners understand*
*and respect each other's needs."*
**— Brené Brown**

Self-care can't survive without boundaries. They aren't punishments, ultimatums, or distance — they're love in structure. A boundary says, "This matters to me, and I want to protect it so I can keep showing up fully for us."

When both partners express and honor boundaries, they create safety — not separation. It's the difference between building walls that isolate and bridges that invite understanding. Boundaries help prevent resentment, protect energy, and remind both people that love grows best where respect and clarity live side by side.

Research supports that healthy boundaries are vital for emotional well-being, fostering trust, authenticity, and mutual respect in relationships (Brown, 2010; Cloud & Townsend, 2017). When partners know and communicate their limits, they strengthen—not threaten—their connection.

## Reflect

Where in your life are your boundaries unclear or often crossed? How does that affect your energy, your mood, or your ability to connect?

What would change if those boundaries were honored—by you and by your partner?

## Engage

Identify one specific area where a boundary could help you protect your self-care this week.

Write it down: _____

_____

_____

_____

## Prompt

"One area where I need clearer boundaries to protect my well-being

is _____. When this boundary is

honored, I feel _____."

## Share

Talk together about how you can both honor these boundaries — without guilt, defensiveness, or resistance. Ask each other: "What helps you feel supported when your boundary is being honored?"

**RelationTip:** Boundaries are a gift. They take the guesswork out of love. When you name what you need, you give your partner the chance to succeed — and that's how trust and peace begin to take root.

# Day 83: Reconnecting After Rest

*"Absence is to love what wind is to fire; it extinguishes the small, it inflames the great."*
— **Roger de Bussy-Rabutin**

Time apart — whether for rest, solitude, or self-care — doesn't weaken love; it refines it. Healthy relationships are like breathing: a rhythm of inhale and exhale, togetherness and space. When we return from rest, we bring back new energy, calm, and perspective that can reignite closeness.

Reconnection isn't about picking up right where you left off — it's about coming back with presence. It's a way of saying, *"I went to refill my cup, and now I want to pour back into us."*

Research on relational rhythms shows that couples who balance autonomy with togetherness report higher satisfaction, emotional stability, and long-term resilience (Girme et al., 2020; Perel, 2006). Rest allows individuality to thrive, while reconnection renews intimacy — the two together create the healthy pulse of love.

## Reflect

When you take space for self-care or reflection, how do you typically re-enter connection with your partner? Do you come back hurried or hesitant? Or do you take time to reconnect intentionally — through touch, conversation, or simple presence? What would it look like to make that transition more mindful?

## Engage

Write down a few small ways you can reconnect after taking time apart. Think of specific gestures, phrases, or rituals that help you and your partner feel close again.

_____

_____

_____

## Prompt

"When I take space to rest, it helps me return to you feeling _____

_____. One way I'd love to reconnect

afterward is _____."

## Share

Talk together about what helps you both feel reconnected after time apart. Maybe it's laughter, conversation, prayer, or physical closeness. Whatever form it takes, let it be a moment of intention — a way to remind each other that space doesn't mean disconnection; it means trust.

**RelationTip:** Rest and reconnection are two sides of the same coin. When you honor both, your love becomes not just durable — but alive.

# Day 84: Reflect on the Progress You've Made

*Tending to yourself is tending to the love that holds you.*

Self-care isn't about routines as much as it is about renewal. Over this past week, you've slowed down, listened to what your body and heart need, and learned that tending to yourself is one of the most relational things you can do. The small shifts you've made—setting boundaries, protecting rest, supporting each other's rhythms—are the quiet foundations of lasting love.

Today, pause to notice what's changed. Where has there been more peace, presence, or ease between you? What moments reminded you that you're both growing not just with each other, but for each other?

Research on relational well-being shows that couples who integrate self-care practices report higher emotional regulation, empathy, and satisfaction (Neff & Germer, 2018; Gottman & Silver, 2015). Reflecting together on growth reinforces those neural pathways of safety and appreciation—the very foundation of secure love.

## Reflect

Think back on the self-care tools and insights from this week.

- What have you learned about yourself?
- How has your partner's self-care inspired or challenged you?
- Where do you feel more grounded or connected than before?

## Engage

List a few tangible ways you've noticed growth in yourself and in your relationship this week. Write short notes or phrases that capture what's different.

_____

_____

_____

## Prompt

"The progress we've made in self-care has strengthened us by _____

_____ because _____

_____."

## Share

End today by celebrating the growth you've witnessed in yourselves and in each other. Acknowledge the ways you've chosen healing over hurry, stillness over striving, and connection over burnout.

**RelationTip:** Self-care is a rhythm, not a reward. Keep tending to yourself and honoring each other's needs — you're not just sustaining love, you're deepening it.

# WEEK 13

# CELEBRATING YOUR GROWTH

# Week 13: Celebrating Your Growth

Congratulations — you've made it to the final week of this journey. What you've done together isn't just commendable; it's sacred. You've shown up when it was hard. You've softened where you once felt stuck. You've dared to be seen, known, and loved more fully.

This week is all about honoring that work — celebrating the miles traveled, the barriers broken, and the love that has grown deeper with every step.

Take a moment to look back — not with shame or judgment, but with gentle curiosity.
Where did you begin? What were you longing for when you started? What fears did you face?
Think of the courage it took to be vulnerable, to name your needs, and to let go of old patterns. You've been *rewiring connection.* You've turned toward each other instead of away. That is no small thing.

Over these past twelve weeks, you've explored emotional safety, conflict repair, empathy, needs, trust, forgiveness, and self-care. You've learned to speak more honestly, listen more intentionally, and repair more quickly. You've discovered that the real work of love often happens in the quiet, daily moments — and that's exactly where it becomes the most beautiful.

This week is about pausing to recognize all of it: the small wins, the breakthroughs, the laughter that returned, and the habits that softened. It's about acknowledging that healing is possible, growth is real, and that your relationship has evolved into something stronger, steadier, and more sacred than before.

As you close this chapter, let this week be a marker — a sacred pause to say: **We did this. We're different. And we're not done growing.**

# Day 85: Honoring How Far You've Come

Take a deep breath and look back. You've traveled far—from uncertainty to understanding, from distance to connection, from reaction to reflection. This journey hasn't been easy. It's taken intention, vulnerability, and courage. But it's also created new tenderness, insight, and safety between you. Today is about pausing to honor that.

You've done the brave work of looking inward and turning toward each other, again and again. That's what healing love looks like—not perfection, but presence.

Research in positive psychology suggests that reflecting on progress and growth amplifies well-being, strengthens motivation, and solidifies emotional bonds (Fredrickson, 2013; Emmons & McCullough, 2003). When couples acknowledge the ground they've gained, they reinforce the neural pathways of gratitude and belonging that keep love resilient.

## Reflect

Think back to where you were when this began.

- How did you feel at the start?
- What were you longing for, hoping for, or even afraid of?
- Now, what feels different—in you, in your partner, in your connection?

## Engage

Share a few specific moments that stand out as turning points in your journey. These might be breakthroughs, small shifts, or quiet realizations that helped you feel closer or safer. Name them together and take a moment to acknowledge what each one meant.

## Prompt

"One of the most meaningful lessons we've learned during this journey is _____ because
_____."

## Share

Take turns expressing gratitude for each other's courage, commitment, and willingness to grow. Celebrate the quiet evidence of transformation: softer tones, longer hugs, calmer pauses, kinder words. Those are the marks of growth that matter most.

**RelationTip:** Growth rarely announces itself. It shows up quietly—in the way you listen, in the way you stay. Honor that. It means you're healing, together.

# Day 86: Celebrating Small Victories

Healing doesn't happen all at once. It happens in a hundred small moments — the pause before reacting, the soft tone instead of the sharp one, the choice to reach rather than retreat. These are the invisible victories that slowly transform love into something lasting.

Today is about honoring the quiet progress you've made — the subtle shifts that built trust, safety, and understanding over time.

Research from habit formation and relationship science supports this truth: small, consistent changes are the foundation of transformation. Psychologist BJ Fogg (2019) found that tiny habits compound into lasting behavioral shifts, while Gottman's longitudinal studies reveal that micro-moments of connection — turning toward rather than away — are what predict long-term relationship stability and satisfaction (Gottman & Silver, 2015).

## Reflect

Think of the small but meaningful moments that changed your connection.

- When did you listen instead of defend?
- When did you stay curious instead of critical?
- When did you risk vulnerability instead of hiding?

These moments matter. They're the daily bricks of a stronger foundation.

## Engage

Share a few of these moments with your partner. Acknowledge the ways you've each shown growth and grace. Notice how the little things added up to something beautiful.

## Prompt

"One small change that had a big impact on our relationship was
_____ because _____
_____."

## Share

Take time to express gratitude for each other's small but consistent efforts. Celebrate with something simple — a walk, a meal, a shared laugh. Let your presence be the party.

**RelationTip:** Small changes compound over time. Celebrate them, because what feels tiny today often becomes the trust, safety, and love you stand on tomorrow.

# Day 87: Celebrating Milestones

Every love story has its milestones — the moments that mark a shift, a breakthrough, or a step closer to one another. Maybe it was a hard conversation that finally led to understanding, a repaired argument that didn't spiral, or a quiet night when you felt safe again after feeling far apart. These moments deserve to be remembered and celebrated.

They are the markers of your growth — the evidence that love can be both tender and strong.

Couples who intentionally pause to acknowledge milestones deepen their emotional connection and reinforce a shared sense of meaning. According to Dr. John Gottman's research on the Sound Relationship House, celebrating small and large moments together strengthens the couple's "shared meaning system" — the sense of being teammates in a shared life story (Gottman & Silver, 2015). Gratitude researcher Robert Emmons also found that acknowledgment of growth moments sustains relational satisfaction and builds emotional resilience (Emmons & McCullough, 2003).

## Reflect

Think of one or two milestones you've experienced during this journey.

- What made them significant?
- How did they change the way you love or listen?
- What do they reveal about how far you've come?

## Engage

Choose one milestone together that feels especially meaningful right now. Write a few words or phrases that capture why it matters — what it symbolizes for your relationship.

_____

_____

_____

## Prompt

"One milestone that stands out to me is _____ because it reminded me that _____."

## Share

Take turns sharing your reflections. Then, mark the moment in a meaningful way — a toast at dinner, a walk under the stars, a quiet embrace. Let this be your way of saying, _We made it through that. Together._

**RelationTip:** Growth happens in layers. Each milestone is not an endpoint but another step toward deeper trust, love, and security. Celebrate them all.

# Day 88: Revisiting Favorite Exercises

Sometimes the best way to see how far you've come is to walk back to where you began. Revisiting your earlier work isn't about seeing what you got "right" or "wrong." It's about witnessing your growth — hearing how your words sound different now, how your heart feels steadier, how your understanding has deepened.

When you return to these moments with new awareness, you'll realize how much life and love have shifted inside you. The questions haven't changed — but you have.

Research supports this process of reflective revisiting. Studies in narrative therapy show that re-engaging earlier stories through a new lens enhances self-awareness and consolidates emotional growth (White & Epston, 1990; Pennebaker & Smyth, 2016). In relationships, this kind of reflection reinforces shared meaning and strengthens long-term emotional bonds (Gottman & Silver, 2015).

## Reflect

Choose one or two exercises or prompts from earlier in the workbook that were particularly meaningful.

## Engage

Go through the one or two exercise(s) together again. Notice what feels easier, what feels tender, and what feels stronger. Talk about how your understanding, patience, or compassion has expanded since the first time.

## Prompt

"When we first did this exercise, I felt _____

_____, but now I feel _____

_____ because _____

_____."

## Share

Take turns sharing what stood out this time around. Let it be gentle
— not about measuring progress but about noticing growth. End
the exercise by expressing gratitude for the journey you've walked
together.

**RelationTip:** Revisiting past moments with new eyes helps you
see your evolution — not just as partners, but as people who keep
choosing love in deeper and more intentional ways.

# Day 89: Planning for the Future

The work you've done together doesn't end here — it grows with you. Every conversation, every repair, every moment of turning toward each other has planted something lasting. Now it's time to nurture what's been planted.

Today isn't about setting rigid goals — it's about being intentional. It's about asking, *What rhythms, habits, and practices will keep us connected when life gets busy again?*

Couples who establish intentional rituals of connection tend to experience greater long-term satisfaction and resilience. Dr. John and Julie Gottman's research highlights that shared meaning and consistent rituals — like weekly check-ins, gratitude moments, or daily affection — anchor relationships through stress and transition (Gottman & Silver, 2015). Relationship psychologist Dr. Terri Orbuch (2012) similarly found that couples who intentionally maintain curiosity, celebration, and touch report higher fulfillment over decades of marriage.

## Reflect

Think about the tools, insights, and rituals that have helped you most throughout this journey.

- What do you want to keep practicing daily or weekly?
- What routines brought you peace or laughter?
- Which lessons do you never want to forget?

## Engage

Together, create a short list of rituals or rhythms that help you stay connected. These can be small things — a morning coffee together, a nightly check-in, a weekly gratitude text. Choose a few that feel natural and sustainable for the season you're in.

## Prompt

"Moving forward, one commitment I want to keep is _____

_____ because it strengthens our

connection by _____."

## Share

Combine your lists into a shared "relationship commitment plan." Write it on a card, your phone, or a note on the fridge — somewhere you'll see often. Let it serve as a daily reminder of what you've built and the future you're growing toward together.

**RelationTip:** Rituals keep love alive. They transform intention into rhythm. When you commit to small, consistent acts of connection, you're not just maintaining your relationship — you're shaping a future defined by safety, trust, and love that lasts.

# Day 90: Celebratory Date

You've made it — 90 days of showing up, leaning in, and choosing love over avoidance, courage over comfort. That's something worth celebrating.

This isn't just the end of a workbook — it's the continuation of your story, now written with deeper safety, trust, and understanding. You've done brave, beautiful work. Today is about pausing to honor that — and each other.

## Reflect

Think about the moments that defined this journey:

- When did you feel most connected?
- What surprised you about yourself — or your partner?
- What are you most proud of?

Let gratitude rise to the surface. You've earned it.

## Engage

Plan a celebratory date together. It doesn't need to be elaborate — just intentional. It might be your favorite restaurant, a walk along the water, a cozy dinner at home, or a slow morning over coffee.

Let the goal be simple: *connection, reflection, and joy.*

## Prompt

"One of my favorite memories from our journey is _____ _____ because it made me feel ___ _____."

## Share

Take turns expressing gratitude for what this experience has meant. Toast to the work you've done, the love you've deepened, and the life you're still building together.

Speak this truth to one another: *We've changed — and we're still becoming.*

**RelationTip:** Celebration creates meaning. When you honor your progress with presence and gratitude, you anchor growth into memory. Love becomes more than a feeling — it becomes a practice you choose, again and again.

# CONCLUSION

As you arrive at the end of this 90-day journey, pause and take a breath.

What you've done together is rare — and it's sacred. You've chosen to lean in when it would've been easier to lean away. You've softened where you used to protect. You've shown up for yourselves and for each other with courage, honesty, and heart.

These last 90 days have been about more than completing exercises — they've been about transforming the way you love. You've practiced presence, curiosity, forgiveness, and truth-telling. You've created something living: a relationship that breathes, adapts, and grows stronger over time.

At the core of every thriving relationship is safety and security. These aren't luxuries — they are the foundation of love itself. Without safety, trust cannot form. Without trust, vulnerability cannot flourish. And without vulnerability, intimacy cannot deepen.

As Dr. Sue Johnson so beautifully reminds us, *"The bond of love is not a luxury. It's a necessity for human beings to thrive."* (Johnson, 2019)

This bond isn't built on perfection — it's built on repair. It's built on the courage to say, "I was wrong," the humility to listen, and the commitment to keep returning to each other again and again. You've learned how to create that safety through honest communication, healthy boundaries, emotional regulation, and compassion. Keep tending to that ground, and your relationship will continue to bloom.

Remember: love does not move in a straight line. There will be times when you drift, disconnect, or forget what safety feels like. That's okay. It doesn't mean you've failed — it means you're human. In those moments, return to this workbook. Revisit the exercises, the conversations, and the truths that brought you here. These pages can serve as a map back home when life feels disorienting.

As Barbara Fredrickson reminds us, *"Love is not something that happens to us. It is something we create together."* (Fredrickson, 2013)

You've spent these past 90 days creating something together — something lasting. But this is not the finish line. Love is a living practice. The more you invest in it, the more resilient it becomes. The more you nurture it, the more it nurtures you.

If at any point you find yourselves facing challenges too heavy to carry alone, know that seeking help is not a sign of failure — it's a profound act of care. Whether through therapy, a couples intensive, or guided retreat, there is always a path forward. Healing doesn't require perfection; it only requires participation.

Love is not static — it's dynamic, alive, and unfolding. It needs tending. And when you tend to it, it rewards you with presence, laughter, softness, and strength.

Ultimately, your relationship is your safe haven in a world that can feel unpredictable. It's the place you return to for grounding, comfort, and joy. Together, you've built something uniquely yours — a connection that reflects both who you are and who you're becoming. Continue to cherish it. Continue to choose each other.

Amber and I are so deeply grateful that we chose the hard work of healing over the hard work of walking away. Both paths are hard — but only one leads you home. Not every relationship makes it, and that's okay. But for those willing to stay curious, humble, and brave enough to face the patterns that disconnect them — there's always a way forward.

Thank you for trusting us to walk beside you in this journey. We believe love is the most powerful force on earth, and your willingness to do this work is proof of that truth.

If you ever need us again — for guidance, a couples intensive, or simply to reconnect — we're here.
Remember this: love is always worth the effort, and safety is always the heart of connection.

Here's to a future filled with peace, play, and passion.
Here's to a love that feels secure.

## Next Steps: Go Deeper Together

If you've ever thought, *"We need more than talk—we need transformation,"* that's exactly why the *Unstuck 3-Day Intensive* was created.

**At an Unstuck Intensive, you and your partner will:**

- Experience **Emotionally Focused Therapy (EFT)** in real time—learning to identify, express, and respond to each other's deepest emotions in a safe, guided setting.

- Engage in **Experiential Therapy** that goes far beyond talking. You'll move, create, and explore—using **props, art, sound, imagery, and sculpting** to bring hidden emotions and relational patterns into the light.

- Learn how to **track your nervous systems together**, using tools rooted in attachment science and Polyvagal Theory to restore calm and connection.

- Gain a **shared language of safety**, leaving with practical tools to sustain your growth long after you return home.

- Be guided every step by **licensed marriage and family therapist Matt Wade**, whose approach blends evidence-based therapy with creativity, heart, and humor.

This is not traditional talk therapy—it's a **full-body, heart-centered experience** designed to help you rediscover safety, empathy, and intimacy in ways you've never experienced before.

If this workbook awakened something in you, follow that curiosity.

**Scan the QR code** or visit <u>unstucktherapy.org</u> to learn more and schedule your 3-day **Unstuck Intensive**.

Your story isn't finished—it's just getting good.

# REFERENCES

Ainsworth, M. D. S., Blehar, M. C., Waters, E., & Wall, S. (1978). *Patterns of attachment: A psychological study of the strange situation.* Lawrence Erlbaum Associates.

Algoe, S. B. (2012). *Find, remind, and bind: The functions of gratitude in everyday relationships. Social and Personality Psychology Compass*, 6(6), 455-467.

Algoe, S. B., Fredrickson, B. L., & Gable, S. L. (2013). The social functions of the emotion of gratitude via expression. *Emotion, 13*(4), 605–609. https://doi.org/10.1037/a0032701

Bowen, M. (1978). *Family therapy in clinical practice.* Jason Aronson.

Bowlby, J. (1969). *Attachment and loss: Vol. 1. Attachment.* Basic Books.

Bowlby, J. (1988). *A secure base: Parent-child attachment and healthy human development.* Basic Books.

Brault, R. (n.d.). *Enjoy the little things, for one day you may look back and realize they were the big things.* [Quotation].

Brown, B. (2010). *The gifts of imperfection: Let go of who you think you're supposed to be and embrace who you are.* Hazelden.

Brown, B. (2012). *Daring greatly: How the courage to be vulnerable transforms the way we live, love, parent, and lead.* Gotham Books.

Brown, B. (2015). *Rising strong: The reckoning, the rumble, the revolution.* Spiegel & Grau.

Brown, B. (2018). *Dare to lead: Brave work. Tough conversations. Whole hearts.* Random House.

Bussy-Rabutin, R. de. (1669). *Lettres et réflexions* [Letters and reflections]. [Original quotation translated as "Absence is to love what wind is to fire; it extinguishes the small, it inflames the great."]

Chapman, G. (1992). *The five love languages: How to express heartfelt commitment to your mate.* Northfield Publishing.

Chafee, L. (n.d.). *Trust = Time + Consistency.* [Quotation].

Cloud, H., & Townsend, J. (2017). *Boundaries: When to say yes, how to say no to take control of your life.* Zondervan.

Coan, J. A., & Sbarra, D. A. (2015). Social baseline theory: The social regulation of risk and effort. *Current Opinion in Psychology, 1*, 87–91. https://doi.org/10.1016/j.copsyc.2014.12.021

Covey, S. R. (1989). *The 7 habits of highly effective people: Powerful lessons in personal change.* Free Press.

Dana, D. (2018). *The polyvagal theory in therapy: Engaging the rhythm of regulation.* W. W. Norton & Company.

Deci, E. L., & Ryan, R. M. (2000). The "what" and "why" of goal pursuits: Human needs and the self-determination of behavior. *Psychological Inquiry, 11*(4), 227–268. https://doi.org/10.1207/S15327965PLI1104_01

Emmons, R. A., & McCullough, M. E. (2003). Counting blessings versus burdens: An experimental investigation of gratitude and subjective well-being in daily life. *Journal of Personality and Social Psychology, 84*(2), 377–389. https://doi.org/10.1037/0022-3514.84.2.377

Fogg, B. J. (2019). *Tiny habits: The small changes that change everything.* Houghton Mifflin Harcourt.

Fox, G. R., Kaplan, J., Damasio, H., & Damasio, A. (2015). Neural correlates of gratitude. *Frontiers in Psychology*, 6, Article 1491. https://doi.org/10.3389/fpsyg.2015.01491

Fredrickson, B. L. (2001). The role of positive emotions in positive psychology: The broaden-and-build theory of positive emotions. *American Psychologist, 56*(3), 218–226. https://doi.org/10.1037/0003-066X.56.3.218

Fredrickson, B. L. (2004). The broaden-and-build theory of positive emotions. *Philosophical Transactions of the Royal Society of London. Series B: Biological Sciences, 359*(1449), 1367–1377. https://doi.org/10.1098/rstb.2004.1512

Fredrickson, B. L. (2009). *Positivity: Top-notch research reveals the 3-to-1 ratio that will change your life.* Crown Publishers.

Fredrickson, B. L. (2013). *Love 2.0: How our supreme emotion affects everything we feel, think, do, and become.* Hudson Street Press.

Girme, Y. U., Overall, N. C., & Faingataa, S. (2020). "My independence is a gift to you": Relationship satisfaction and autonomy support in romantic relationships. *Journal of Personality and Social Psychology, 118*(3), 497–520. https://doi.org/10.1037/pspi0000181

Gordon, A. M., Impett, E. A., Kogan, A., Oveis, C., & Keltner, D. (2012). To have and to hold: Gratitude promotes relationship maintenance in intimate bonds. *Personal Relationships*, 19(2), 217-233.

**Gottman, J. M., & Gottman, J. S. (2017).** *Eight dates: Essential conversations for a lifetime of love.* Workman Publishing.

Gottman, J. M., & DeClaire, J. (2001). *The relationship cure: A 5 step guide to strengthening your marriage, family, and friendships.* Harmony Books.

Gottman, J. M., & Silver, N. (1999). *The seven principles for making marriage work.* Harmony Books.

Gottman, J. M., & Silver, N. (2015). *What makes love last? How to build trust and avoid betrayal.* Simon & Schuster.

Hemphill, P. (2018, November 15). *Boundaries are the distance at which I can love you and me simultaneously* [Tweet]. Twitter. https://twitter.com/prentishemphill/status/1063192585771794432

Johnson, S. M. (2008). *Hold me tight: Seven conversations for a lifetime of love.* Little, Brown and Company.

Johnson, S. M. (2013). *Love sense: The revolutionary new science of romantic relationships.* Little, Brown Spark.

Johnson, S. M. (2019). *Attachment theory in practice: Emotionally focused therapy (EFT) with individuals, couples, and families.* Guilford Press.

Kerr, M. E., & Bowen, M. (1988). *Family evaluation: An approach based on Bowen theory.* W. W. Norton & Company.

Lally, P., van Jaarsveld, C. H. M., Potts, H. W. W., & Wardle, J. (2010). *How are habits formed: Modelling habit formation in the real world.* European Journal of Social Psychology, 40(6), 998–1009. https://doi.org/10.1002/ejsp.674

Lambert, N. M., & Fincham, F. D. (2011). Expressing gratitude to a partner leads to more relationship maintenance behavior. *Emotion, 11*(1), 52–60. https://doi.org/10.1037/a0021557

Lamott, A. (1994). *Bird by bird: Some instructions on writing and life.* Anchor Books.

Lamott, A. (1999). *Traveling mercies: Some thoughts on faith.* Anchor Books.
(Note: Source of the quotation "Almost everything will work again if you unplug it for a few minutes, including you.")

Lamott, A. (2018). *Almost everything: Notes on hope.* Riverhead Books.

Lerner, H. G. (2005). *The dance of connection: How to talk to someone when you're mad, hurt, scared, frustrated, insulted, betrayed, or desperate.* HarperCollins.

Main, M., & Solomon, J. (1990). *Procedures for identifying infants as disorganized/disoriented during the Ainsworth Strange Situation.* In M. T. Greenberg, D. Cicchetti, & E. M. Cummings (Eds.), *Attachment in the preschool years: Theory, research, and intervention* (pp. 121–160). University of Chicago Press.

Maritain, J. (1962). *Reflections on gratitude and courtesy.* [Quotation, commonly attributed to Maritain: "Gratitude is the most exquisite form of courtesy."]

Mellody, P., Miller, A. W., & Miller, J. K. (1992). *Facing love addiction: Giving yourself the power to change the way you love.* HarperCollins.
(Note: Source for the definition of intimacy as sharing your own reality and receiving another's without judgment.)

Neff, K. (2011). *Self-compassion: The proven power of being kind to yourself.* William Morrow.
(Note: Source of "treating yourself with the same care and understanding you would offer a good friend.")

Neff, K. D., & Germer, C. K. (2018). *The mindful self-compassion workbook: A proven way to accept yourself, build inner strength, and thrive.* Guilford Press.

Orbuch, T. L. (2012). *Finding love again: 6 simple steps to a new and happy relationship.* Sourcebooks Casablanca.

Pennebaker, J. W., & Smyth, J. M. (2016). *Opening up by writing it down: How expressive writing improves health and eases emotional pain* (3rd ed.). Guilford Press.

Perel, E. (2006). *Mating in captivity: Unlocking erotic intelligence.* HarperCollins.

Perel, E. (2017). *The state of affairs: Rethinking infidelity.* HarperCollins.

Porges, S. W. (2011). *The polyvagal theory: Neurophysiological foundations of emotions, attachment, communication, and self-regulation.* W. W. Norton & Company.

Reis, H. T., O'Keefe, S. D., & Lane, R. D. (2018). Fun is more fun when we do it together: The social regulation of emotion. In J. J. Gross (Ed.), *Handbook of emotion regulation* (2nd ed., pp. 263–280). The Guilford Press.

Rogers, C. R. (1961). *On becoming a person: A therapist's view of psychotherapy.* Houghton Mifflin.

Rosenberg, M. B. (2015). *Nonviolent communication: A language of life* (3rd ed.). PuddleDancer Press.

Schnarch, D. M. (1997). *Passionate marriage: Keeping love and intimacy alive in committed relationships.* W. W. Norton & Company.

Shaver, P. R., & Mikulincer, M. (2002). *Attachment-related psychodynamics.* Attachment & Human Development, 4(2), 133–161. https://doi.org/10.1080/14616730210154171

Siegel, D. J. (2010). *The mindful therapist: A clinician's guide to mindsight and neural integration.* W. W. Norton & Company.

**Siegel, D. J. (2012).** *The developing mind: How relationships and the brain interact to shape who we are* (2nd ed.). Guilford Press.

Tatkin, S. (2012). *Wired for love: How understanding your partner's brain and attachment style can help you defuse conflict and build a secure relationship.* New Harbinger Publications.

The Forgiveness Project. (n.d.). *On forgiveness and the impact of letting go of resentment.* The Forgiveness Project.
(Note: Referenced for physiological and psychological benefits of forgiveness, including reduced stress, blood pressure, and improved heart health.)

Tronick, E. Z. (2007). *The neurobehavioral and social-emotional development of infants and children.* W. W. Norton & Company.
(Note: Referenced for misattunement, repair, and co-regulation, including the Still-Face paradigm.)

Ward, W. A. (1972). *Thoughts of a Christian optimist: The words of William Arthur Ward.* Droke House.
(Note: Source for "Feeling gratitude and not expressing it is like wrapping a present and not giving it." and "Gratitude turns ordinary days into thanksgiving...")

White, M., & Epston, D. (1990). *Narrative means to therapeutic ends.* W. W. Norton & Company.

Wood, W. (2019). *Good habits, bad habits: The science of making positive changes that stick.* Farrar, Straus and Giroux.

Winfrey, O. (2010). *Oprah on forgiveness.* [Public talk / interview transcript]. Harpo Productions.
(Note: Source of "Forgiveness is giving up the hope that the past could have been any different.")